The New Depression

The New Depression

The Breakdown of the Paper Money Economy

RICHARD DUNCAN

WILEY

John Wiley & Sons Singapore Pte. Ltd.

Other Wiley Editorial Offices
John Wiley & Sons, 111 River Street, Hoboken, NJ 07030, USA
John Wiley & Sons, The Atrium, Southern Gate, Chichester, West Sussex, P019 8SQ, United Kingdom
John Wiley & Sons (Canada) Ltd., 5353 Dundas Street West, Suite 400, Toronto, Ontario, M9B 6HB, Canada
John Wiley & Sons Australia Ltd., 42 McDougall Street, Milton, Queensland 4064, Australia
Wiley-VCH, Boschstrasse 12, D-69469 Weinheim, Germany

ISBN 978–1–118–15779–4 (Hardback)
ISBN 978–1–118–15780–0 (ePDF)
ISBN 978–1–118–15781–7 (Mobi)
ISBN 978–1–118–15782–4 (ePub)

Typeset in 10/12pt, ITC Garamond by MPS Limited, Chennai, India

10 9 8 7 6 5 4 3 2

Contents

Preface   *ix*

CHAPTER 1   How Credit Slipped Its Leash   1

Opening Pandora's Box   1
Constraints on the Fed and on Paper Money Creation   3
Fractional Reserve Banking Run Amok   5
Fractional Reserve Banking   5
Commercial Banks   7
The Broader Credit Market: Too Many Lenders,
   Not Enough Reserves   10
Credit without Reserves   12
The Flow of Funds   13
The Rest of the World   15
Notes   15

CHAPTER 2   The Global Money Glut   17

The Financial Account   18
How It Works   20
What Percentage of Total Foreign Exchange
   Reserves Are Dollars?   23
What to Do with So Many Dollars?   24
What about the Remaining $2.8 Trillion?   26
Debunking the Global Savings Glut Theory   28
Will China Dump Its Dollars?   31
Notes   32

CHAPTER 3   Creditopia   33

Who Borrowed the Money?   33
Impact on the Economy   38
Net Worth   39
Profits   41
Tax Revenue   41
Different, Not Just More   41
Impact on Capital   45
Conclusion   49
Note   49

CHAPTER 4   The Quantity Theory of Credit   51

The Quantity Theory of Money   52
The Rise and Fall of Monetarism   55
The Quantity Theory of Credit   57
Credit and Inflation   59
Conclusion   60
Notes   61

CHAPTER 5   The Policy Response: Perpetuating the Boom   63

The Credit Cycle   64
How Have They Done so Far?   65
Monetary Omnipotence and the Limits Thereof   66
The Balance Sheet of the Federal Reserve   67
Quantitative Easing: Round One   69
What Did QE1 Accomplish?   71
Quantitative Easing: Round Two   72
Monetizing the Debt   73
The Role of the Trade Deficit   75
Diminishing Returns   76
The Other Money Makers   78
Notes   83

CHAPTER 6   Where Are We Now?   85

How Bad so Far?   85
Credit Growth Drove Economic Growth   86

So, Where Does that Leave Us? 88
Why Can't TCMD Grow? 89
The Banking Industry: Why Still Too
   Big to Fail? 96
Global Imbalances: Still Unresolved 101
Vision and Leadership Are Still Lacking 104
Notes 105

CHAPTER 7   How It Plays Out 107

The Business Cycle 107
Debt: Public and Private 109
2011: The Starting Point 111
2012: Expect QE3 112
Impact on Asset Prices 114
2013–2014: Three Scenarios 114
Impact on Asset Prices 118
Conclusion 119
Notes 120

CHAPTER 8   Disaster Scenarios 121

The Last Great Depression 121
And This Time? 126
Banking Crisis 126
Protectionism 127
Geopolitical Consequences 128
Conclusion 132
Note 132

CHAPTER 9   The Policy Options 133

Capitalism and the Laissez-Faire Method 134
The State of Government Finances 140
The Government's Options 142
American Solar 143
Conclusion 146
Notes 147

CHAPTER 10   Fire and Ice, Inflation and Deflation   149

Fire   150
Ice   151
Fisher's Theory of Debt-Deflation   152
Winners and Losers   155
Ice Storm   157
Fire Storm   157
Wealth Preservation through Diversification   158
Other Observations Concerning Asset Prices in the
    Age of Paper Money   160
Protectionism and Inflation   165
Consequences of Regulating Derivatives   166
Conclusion   166
Notes   167

Conclusion   *169*
About the Author   *171*
Index   *173*

Preface

When the United States removed the gold backing from the dollar in 1968, the nature of money changed. The result was a proliferation of credit that not only transformed the size and structure of the U.S. economy but also brought about a transformation of the economic system itself. The production process ceased to be driven by saving and investment as it had been since before the Industrial Revolution. Instead, borrowing and consumption began to drive the economic dynamic. Credit creation replaced capital accumulation as the vital force in the economic system.

Credit expanded 50 times between 1964 and 2007. So long as it expanded, prosperity increased. Asset prices rose. Jobs were created. Profits soared. Then, in 2008, credit began to contract, and the economic system that was founded on and sustained by credit was hurled into crisis. It was then that the New Depression began.

There is a grave danger that the credit-based economic paradigm that has shaped the global economy for more than a generation will now collapse. The inability of the private sector to bear any additional debt strongly suggests that this paradigm has reached and exceeded its capacity to generate growth through further credit expansion. If credit contracts significantly and debt deflation takes hold, this economic system will break down in a scenario resembling the 1930s, a decade that began in economic disaster and ended in geopolitical catastrophe.

This book sets out to provide a comprehensive explanation of this crisis. It begins by explaining the developments that allowed credit in the United States to expand 50 times in less than 50 years. Chapter 1, How Credit Slipped Its Leash, looks at the domestic causes. Chapter 2, The Global Money Glut, describes the foreign causes, debunking Fed Chairman Bernanke's global savings glut theory along the way. Chapter 3, Creditopia, discusses how $50 trillion of credit transformed the U.S. economy.

Chapter 4, The Quantity Theory of Credit, is introduced. This theory explains the relationship between credit and economic output. Therefore, it is an indispensible tool for understanding every aspect of this credit-induced calamity: its causes, the government's response to the crisis, and its probable evolution over the years ahead.

Chapter 5, Perpetuating the Boom, explains the government's policy response to the crisis. When seen through the framework of the quantity theory of credit, the rationale for the stimulus packages, the bank bailouts, and the multiple rounds of quantitative easing becomes obvious: the government is desperate to prevent credit from contracting.

Chapter 6, Where Are We Now?, takes stock of the current state of the economy. It looks at each sector of the U.S. economy to determine which ones, if any, can expand their debt further. Economic growth has come to depend on credit expansion. Therefore, if none of the major sectors is capable of taking on more debt, the economy cannot grow. This chapter also considers whether any of the imbalances and mistakes that led to this systemic crisis has yet been eliminated.

Chapter 7, How It Plays Out, presents scenarios of how events are most likely to evolve between the end of 2011 and the end of 2014, along with a discussion of how asset prices would be impacted under each scenario. Chapter 8, Disaster Scenarios, describes how bad things could become if the United States' credit-based economic system breaks down altogether. Its purpose is to make clear just how high the stakes really are, in the belief—the hope—that nothing focuses the mind like the hangman's noose.

Chapter 9, The Policy Options, discusses the novel and unappreciated possibilities inherent in an economic system built on credit and dependent on credit expansion for its survival. This crisis came about because the credit that has been extended was primarily wasted on consumption. Disaster may be averted if the United States now borrows to invest.

The final chapter, Fire and Ice, explains that the U.S. economy could experience high rates of inflation, severe deflation, or both as this crisis unfolds during the years ahead; and it discusses how stocks, bonds, commodities, and currencies would be affected under each scenario. In this post-capitalist age of paper money, government policy will determine the direction in which asset prices move.

The New Depression has not yet become the New Great Depression. Tragically, the odds are increasing that it will. Fiat money has a long and ignoble history of generating economic calamities. The price the United States ultimately pays for abandoning sound money may be devastatingly high, both economically and politically.

CHAPTER 1

How Credit Slipped Its Leash

Irredeemable paper money has almost invariably proved a curse to the country employing it.

—Irving Fisher[1]

Credit-induced boom and bust cycles are not new. What makes this one so extraordinary is the magnitude of the credit expansion that fed it. Throughout most of the twentieth century, two important constraints limited how much credit could be created in the United States. The legal requirement that the Federal Reserve hold gold to back the paper currency it issued was the first. The legal requirement that commercial banks hold liquidity reserves to back their deposits was the second. This chapter describes how those constraints were removed, allowing credit to expand to an extent that economists of earlier generations would have found inconceivable.

Opening Pandora's Box

In February 1968, President Lyndon Johnson asked Congress to end the requirement that dollars be backed by gold. He said:

> *The gold reserve requirement against Federal Reserve notes is not needed to tell us what prudent monetary policy should be—that myth was destroyed long ago.*
>
> *It is not needed to give value to the dollar—that value derives from our productive economy.*[2]

The following month Congress complied.

EXHIBIT 1.1 Money, Credit, and GDP

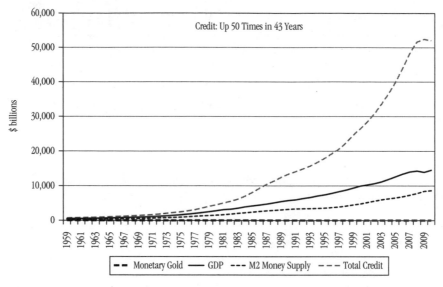

Source: Federal Reserve

That decision fundamentally altered the nature of money in the United States and permitted an unprecedented proliferation of credit. Exhibit 1.1 dramatically illustrates what has occurred.

The monetary gold line at the bottom of the chart represents the gold held within the banking system. It peaked at $19 billion in 1959 and afterward contracted to $10 billion by 1971. M2 represents the money supply as defined as currency held by the public, bank liquidity reserves, and deposits at commercial banks. The top line represents total credit in the country.

It is immediately apparent that credit expanded dramatically both in absolute terms and relative to gold in the banking system and to the money supply. In 1968, the ratio of credit to gold was 128 times and the ratio of credit to the money supply was 2.4 times. By 2007, those ratios had expanded to more than 4,000 times and 6.6 times, respectively. Notice, also, the extraordinary expansion of the ratio of credit to GDP. In 1968, credit exceeded GDP by 1.5 times. In 2007, the amount of credit in the economy had grown to 3.4 times total economic output.

Total credit in the United States surpassed $1 trillion for the first time in 1964. Over the following 43 years, it increased 50 times to $50 trillion in 2007. That explosion of credit changed the world.

Constraints on the Fed and on Paper Money Creation

The Federal Reserve Act of 1913 created the Federal Reserve System and gave it the power to issue Federal Reserve Notes (i.e., paper currency). However, that Act required the Fed to hold "reserves in gold of not less than forty per centum against its Federal Reserve notes in actual circulation."[3] In other words, the central bank was required to hold 40 cents worth of gold for each paper dollar it issued. In 1945, Congress reduced that ratio from 40 percent to 25 percent.

So much gold had flowed into U.S. banks during the second half of the 1930s as the result of political instability in Europe that the Federal Reserve had no difficulty meeting the required ratio of gold to currency for decades. In fact, in 1949, it held nearly enough gold to fully back every Federal Reserve note in circulation.

During the 1950s and 1960s, however, the amount of gold held by the Fed declined. From a peak of $24.4 billion in 1949, the Fed's gold holdings fell to $19.4 billion in 1959 and to only $10.3 billion in 1968. Moreover, not only was the gold stock contracting, the currency in circulating was increasing at a significantly faster pace. During the 1950s, currency in circulation grew at an average rate of 1.5 percent a year, but by an average of 4.7 percent a year during the 1960s.

In 1968, the ratio of the Fed's gold to currency in circulation declined to 25 percent (as shown in Exhibit 1.2), the level it was required to maintain by law. At that point, Congress, at the urging of President Johnson, removed that binding constraint entirely with the passage of the Gold Reserve Requirement Elimination Act of 1968. Afterward, the Fed was no longer required to hold any gold to back its Federal Reserve notes. Had the law not changed, either the Fed would have had to stop issuing new paper currency or else it would have had to acquire more gold.

Once dollars were no longer backed by gold, the nature of money changed. The worth of the currency in circulation was no longer derived from a real asset with intrinsic value. In other words, it was no longer commodity money. It had become fiat money—that is, it was money only because the government said it was money. There was no constraint on how much money of this kind the government could create. And, in the years that followed, the fiat money supply exploded.

Between 1968 and 2010, the Fed increased the number of these paper dollars in circulation by 20 times by printing $886 billion worth of new Federal Reserve notes. (See Exhibit 1.3.) (Its gold holdings now amount to the equivalent of 1 percent of the Federal Reserves notes in circulation.)

Although this new paper money was no longer backed by gold (or by anything at all), it still served as the foundation upon which new credit could be created by the banking system. Fifty trillion dollars worth of credit could not have been erected on the 1968 base of 44 billion gold-backed dollars.

EXHIBIT 1.2 The Ratio of the Fed's Gold Holdings to Currency Outside Banks

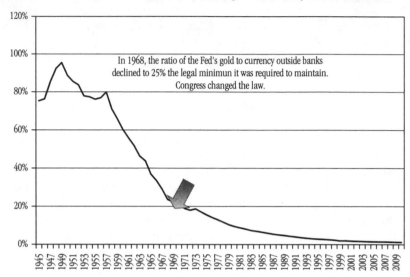

Source: Federal Reserve, Flow of Funds

EXHIBIT 1.3 Currency Outside Banks

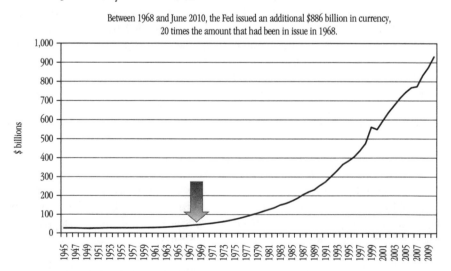

Source: Federal Reserve, Flow of Funds

Fractional Reserve Banking Run Amok

The other constraint on credit creation at the time the Federal Reserve was established was the requirement that banks hold reserves to ensure they would have sufficient liquidity to repay their customers' deposits on demand. The Federal Reserve Act specified that banks must hold such reserves either in their own vaults or else as deposits at the Federal Reserve.

The global economic crisis came about because, over time, regulators lowered the amount of reserves the financial system was required to hold until they were so small that they provided next to no constraint on the amount of credit the system could create. The money multiplier expanded toward infinity. A proliferation of credit created an economic boom that transformed not only the size and composition of the U.S. economy but also the size and composition of the global economy. The collapse came when the borrowers became too heavily indebted to repay what they had borrowed.

By 2007, the reserves ratio of the financial system as a whole had become so small that the amount of credit that the system created was far beyond anything the world had experienced before. By the turn of the century, the reserve requirement played practically no role whatsoever in constraining credit creation. This came about due to two changes in the regulation of the financial industry. The first was a reduction of the amount of reserves that banks were required to hold. The second was regulatory approval that allowed new types of creditors to enter the industry with little to no mandatory reserve requirements whatsoever. The following pages describe this evolution of the U.S. financial industry.

In order to understand how reserve requirements limited credit creation, it is first necessary to understand how credit is created through Fractional Reserve Banking.

Fractional Reserve Banking

Most banks around the world accept deposits, set aside a part of those deposits as reserves, and lend out the rest. Banks hold reserves to ensure they have sufficient funds available to repay their customers' deposits upon demand. To fail to do so could result in a bank run and possibly the failure of the bank. In some countries, banks are legally bound to hold such reserves, while in others they are not. A banking system in which banks do not maintain 100 percent reserves for their deposits is known as a system of *fractional reserve banking*. In such a system, by lending a multiple of the reserves they keep on hand, banks are said to create deposits.

The following example illustrates how the process of deposit creation occurs. In this example, it is assumed that the country in which the banking system operates is on a gold standard, and that banks in that country are required to hold a level of gold reserves equivalent to 20 percent of their deposits.

The process begins when Bank A accepts a deposit of $100 worth of gold. To meet the 20 percent reserve requirement, it sets aside $20 in gold as reserves. It then lends out the remaining $80. The recipient of the loan deposits the $80 into his bank, Bank B. Bank B sets aside 20 percent of the $80, or $16 worth of gold, as reserves. It lends out $64, which ends up in Bank C. This process occurs again and again (see Exhibit 1.4). Therefore, an initial deposit of $100 worth of gold, through the magic of fractional reserve banking, eventually leaves the banking system with $500 of deposits and $400 of credit, while an amount equivalent to the initial deposit is set aside as $100 worth of reserves. The balance sheet of the banking sector would show assets of $500, made up of $400 in loans plus $100 in reserves; and it would show liabilities of $500 made up entirely of deposits.

EXHIBIT 1.4 "Money Creation" through Fractional Reserve Banking
Assuming:
An initial deposit of $100 of gold
A Reserve Ratio of 20%

	Deposits	Reserves	Loans
Round 1	100	20	80
Round 2	80	16	64
Round 3	64	13	51
Round 4	51	10	41
Round 5	41	8	33
Round 6	33	7	26
Round 7	26	5	21
Round 8	21	4	17
Round 9	17	3	13
Round 10	13	3	11
Round 11	11	2	9
Round 12	9	2	7
Round 30	0.2	0.0	0.1
Round 31	0.1	0.0	0.1
Total	500	100	400

In the real world, there are a number of other factors that would have to be taken into consideration. Nevertheless, this simplified example is sufficient to demonstrate the process of deposit creation.

There are two important points to grasp here. First, fractional reserve banking creates credit as well deposits. In the previous example, $400 worth of credit was created by the banking system. Second, the reserve ratio is the factor that determines the maximum amount of deposits (and credit) that can be created. In this example, at the end of the process, there are $500 of deposits, or five times the amount of gold initially deposited, and $400 of credit that did not exist before. The inverse of the reserve requirement is known as the *money multiplier*. Here, the money multiplier is 1/20 percent or 5 times. If the reserve requirement had been 10 percent, the banking system would have ended up with $1,000 of deposits, or 10 times the amount of gold initially deposited, and $900 of new credit. In that case the money multiplier would be 10.

Now consider the reduction of the reserve requirements of the commercial banks.

Commercial Banks

Commercial banking was a straightforward business after the passage of the Glass–Steagall Act separated commercial banking from investment banking in 1933. Banks took deposits and used them to make loans; and the banks were required to hold reserves with the central bank to ensure they would have sufficient liquidity to repay deposits to their customers upon demand. In 1945, deposits supplied 98 percent of the banks' funding. The legal reserve requirement was 20 percent for demand deposits (which accounted for 76 percent of funding) and 6 percent for time deposits (22 percent of funding). Those reserve requirements could be met by a combination of cash held in the banks' vaults and reserves deposited with the central bank.[4] (*Note:* The Reserve requirement on demand deposits for country banks was lower, 14 percent.)

Over time, banks began to rely more heavily on time deposits, which required fewer reserves. By 2007, demand deposits amounted to only 6 percent of commercial banks' funding. Time deposits had increased to 57 percent of funding. This alone significantly reduced the amount of money that banks had to keep as reserves. In addition to accepting deposits, the banks had begun to raise funds by selling commercial paper and bonds, as well as by borrowing in the repo market. In 2007, 12 percent of the banks' funding came from issuing credit market instruments, 8 percent from the repo market, and 17 percent from *miscellaneous liabilities.* They were not required to set aside any reserves against those types of liabilities.

Furthermore, over the decades, the Fed had also repeatedly lowered the amount of reserves that banks were required to hold against both demand and time deposits. Currently, reserve requirements are set out as follows:

- For net transactions accounts of less than $10.7 million, 0 percent
- For those between $10.7 and $58.8 million, 3 percent
- For those greater than $58.8 million, 10 percent

No reserves are required for nonpersonal time deposits.[5] Combined, these developments left the banks with a level of reserves so small as to be practically meaningless when the crisis of 2008 occurred.

In 1945, commercial banks had held reserves and vault cash of $17.8 billion, the equivalent of 12 percent of their total assets, at a time when 64 percent of their assets were (very low risk) U.S. government bonds. By 2007, the banks' reserves and vault cash had tripled to $73.2 billion, but their assets had increased by 82 times to $11.9 trillion. That put the liquidity ratio at 0.6 percent.

The amount of reserves the banks held at the Fed was only $2 billion larger in 2007 than it had been in 1945; and almost all the increase in vault cash resulted from the cash held in the "vaults" of the banks' automatic teller machines. (See Exhibit 1.5.)

EXHIBIT 1.5 Commercial Bank's Reserves at the Federal Reserve, 1945 to 2007

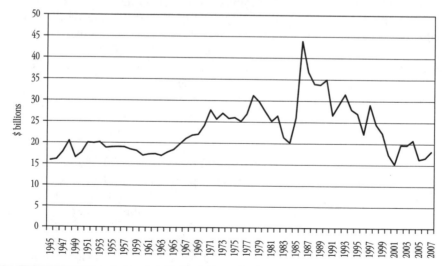

Source: Federal Reserve, Flow of Funds

Beginning in 1988, banks were required to maintain a *capital adequacy ratio* (CAR) of 8 percent. The "capital" supplying the banks' capital adequacy was not a pool of liquid assets, however. It was essentially just a bookkeeping entry representing the difference between the banks' assets and liabilities. The capital was put to work by the banks, either being extended as loans or else invested in credit instruments. Since the capital could be used to make loans, it did not constrain credit creation the way liquidity reserves (held as physical cash or separated and held on deposit at the central bank) had done. Moreover, as described next, although the quantity of the industry's capital increased over time, the quality of that capital deteriorated sharply.

The Fed justified reducing the banks' reserves requirements on the grounds that they were no longer necessary because the Fed itself would always be able to provide liquidity support to any bank that required short-term funding. Clearly, the Fed did not understand the consequences of its actions. By reducing the banks' reserve requirements, the Fed enabled the commercial banks to create much more credit than otherwise would have been possible. The ratio of commercial bank assets to reserves and vault cash exploded from 8 times in 1945 to 162 times in 2007. Conversely, the ratio of their reserves and vault cash to liabilities plummeted. (See Exhibit 1.6.) In the end, when the crisis came, the Fed did provide the banks with the liquidity they required. But to do so, it had to create $1.7 trillion of new fiat money, an amount equivalent to 12 percent of the U.S. GDP. That rescue operation became known as *quantitative easing, round one* (QE1). It will be described in greater detail in Chapter 5.

EXHIBIT 1.6 Commercial Banks' Vault Cash and Reserves to Total Liabilities, 1945 to 2007

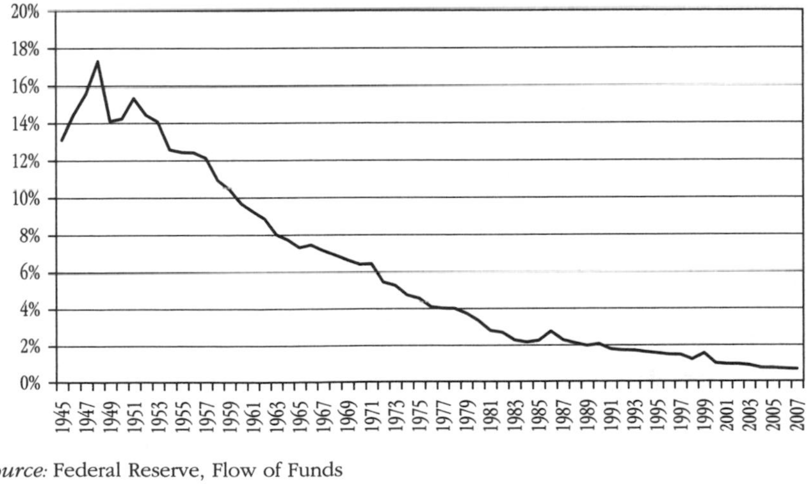

Source: Federal Reserve, Flow of Funds

The Broader Credit Market: Too Many Lenders, Not Enough Reserves

As the reserve requirements of the commercial banks fell and the money multiplier expanded, credit creation through fractional reserve banking exploded. But that is only part of the story. Starting in the 1970s, the structure of the financial system in the United States changed radically. Many new types of credit providers emerged, and, in most cases, the new lending institutions were not subject to any reserve requirements whatsoever.

Exhibit 1.7 provides a snapshot of the country's credit structure in 1945 and in 2007.

At the end of World War II, the credit structure of the United States was simple and straightforward. It became vastly more complicated and leveraged, however, as time went by and new kinds of financial entities were permitted to extend credit.

In 1945, the household sector supplied 26 percent of the country's credit. Households had invested heavily in government bonds during the war.

The financial sector supplied 64 percent of all credit. At that time, commercial banks dominated the financial industry, providing 33 percent of all the credit in the country. Life insurance companies supplied 12 percent of total credit, and other savings institutions, such as thrifts and savings & loan companies, accounted for a further 7 percent. These three sets of financial

EXHIBIT 1.7 Total Credit Market Debt Held by the Creditors

	1945	2007
Total $ billions	$355	$50,043
Household Sector	26%	8%
Financial Sector	64%	73%
including:		
Commercial banks	33%	18%
Life insurance companies	12%	6%
Savings institutions	7%	3%
GSEs & GSE-backed mortgages	1%	15%
Issuers of asset-backed securities	0%	9%
Money market funds	0%	4%
Mutual funds	0%	4%
Others financial sector	11%	14%
Rest of the World	1%	15%
Miscellaneous	9%	4%
	100%	100%

Source: Federal Reserve, Flow of Funds

institutions were all tightly regulated by the government in a way that ensured their risks were limited and their liquidity was ample.

By 2007, the relative importance of each of those three groups had been roughly cut in half. Of all the credit supplied in the country, commercial banks provided 18 percent, life insurance companies provided 6 percent, and the savings institutions provided 3 percent. New financial institutions had emerged as important creditors, and they had eroded the market share of the traditional lenders.

Fannie Mae, Freddie Mac, and other government-sponsored enterprises (GSEs) began growing aggressively during the 1980s. Their mission was to make housing more affordable. To accomplish that mission, those government-backed entities issued debt and used the proceeds to buy mortgage loans from banks and other mortgage originators, who then had the resources to extend more mortgages.

By 1985, the GSEs overtook life insurance companies as the third largest credit provider within the financial sector. Five years later, they moved into second place, overtaking the savings institutions. In 2002, they came very close to overtaking commercial banks as well. In other words, they came very close to being the largest suppliers of credit in the United States. (See Exhibit 1.8.)

Issuers of *asset-backed securities* (ABSs) also became major credit providers. ABS issuers acquired funding by selling bonds. They used the

EXHIBIT 1.8 The Suppliers of Credit from the Financial Sector

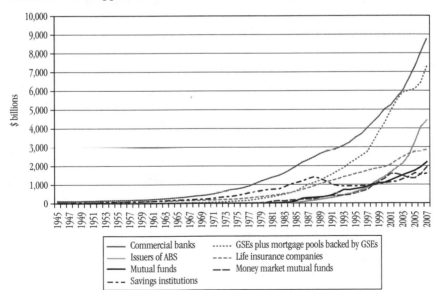

Source: Federal Reserve, Flow of Funds

proceeds to buy mortgage loans, credit card loans, student loans, and some other credit instruments, which they then bundled together in a variety of ways and sold to investors as investment vehicles with different degrees of credit risk. They were not significant players in the credit markets until the second half of the 1980s. By 2007, however, ABS issuers supplied 12 percent of the credit provided by the financial sector or 9 percent of all credit outstanding.

Mutual funds and money market funds had also come of age during the 1980s, and by 2007, they provided 6 percent and 5 percent, respectively, of all credit supplied by the financial sector.

Credit without Reserves

By 2007, the GSEs and the issuers of ABSs provided 24 percent of all the credit in the country. Their rise made the financial system much more leveraged and complex than when it had been dominated by the commercial banks. First of all, the GSEs and ABS issuers faced much lower capital adequacy requirements than the traditional lenders. Banks and savings institutions were required to maintain capital equivalent to 8 percent of their assets—in other words, a CAR of 8 percent. Life insurance companies were also tightly regulated and made to keep large capital reserves. Fannie and Freddie, however, were required to hold only 2.5 percent capital against the mortgage loans held on their books and only 0.45 percent for the mortgages they had guaranteed. Fannie, for example, in 2007 had assets (mortgages and guarantees) valued at $2.9 trillion, but shareholders' funds (capital) of only $44 billion. Therefore, Fannie's CAR (equity to assets) was only 1.5 percent. Freddie's was even less, 1.3 percent that year.

The case of the ABS issuers was similar. Generally, the issuers of ABSs were special purpose vehicles (SPVs) that had been created for the purpose of packaging and selling loans that had been originated by commercial banks, investments banks, or corporations such as General Electric and Chrysler. Moving assets into the SPVs reduced the amount of capital the loan originators were required to hold, even though quite often the originators remained the beneficial owners of the SPVs. For example, holding mortgage-backed securities with AAA or AA ratings required only 1.6 percent capital backing. And, generally, the credit rating agencies were happy to provide such a rating—for a fee. Therefore, ABS issuers held much lower CARs than the banks did.

More importantly, the GSEs and ABS issuers faced no liquidity reserve requirements at all. They raised funding by issuing debt and, in the process of issuing debt, they created credit. Fannie Mae and Freddie Mac alone owned nearly $5 trillion in mortgage assets at the end of 2007. They had funded the purchases of those mortgages by issuing roughly $5 trillion in Fannie and Freddie bonds, an amount equivalent in size to 10 percent of the entire credit market.

Just as commercial banks created credit by making loans (through the system of fractional reserves banking), the GSEs and ABS issuers also created credit by extending credit—but with even less constraint because they were not required to hold any liquidity reserves. Rather than remaining a system of fractional reserve banking, the financial system of the United States had evolved into one entirely unconstrained by reserve requirements. Consequently, there was no limit as to how much credit that system could create.

The events of 2008 brutally revealed the gross inadequacy of the financial system's capital and liquidity.

The Flow of Funds

The Fed's Flow of Funds Accounts provides a near-comprehensive set of information about the stock and flow of credit in the United States. Because credit growth now drives economic growth, the flow of funds is the key to understanding developments in the U.S. economy.

The *Flow of Funds Accounts of the United States* is published by the Federal Reserves on its website each quarter at www.federalreserve.gov/releases/z1/Current/z1.pdf.

Credit and debt are two sides of the same coin. One person's debt is another person's asset. As of June 30, 2011, the total size of the U.S. credit market was $52.6 trillion. Throughout this book, this figure is referred to as *total credit market debt,* or TCMD.

Table L.1 of the *Flow of Funds* report, titled Credit Market Debt Outstanding, is the summary table of TCMD. It provides a breakdown by sector of (1) who owes the debt, "Total credit market debt owed by" and (2) to whom the debt is owed, "Total credit market assets held by."

The top half of Table L.1, the breakdown of who owes the debt, has been provided as Exhibit 1.9. There are three major categories:

1. The domestic nonfinancial sectors
2. The rest of the world
3. The financial sectors

Note: Detailed information on each of these categories, as well as details concerning who owns the debt, can be found in the other 144 tables spread across the *Flow of Funds Accounts of the United States.* All

EXHIBIT 1.9 Credit Market Debt Outstanding
L.1 Credit Market Debt Outstanding
Billions of dollars

		2006	2007	2008	2009	2010
1	**Total Credit Market Debt Owed by:**	45,354	50,043	52,433	52,266	52,399
2	**Domestic nonfinancial sectors**	29,180	31,699	33,602	34,634	36,113
3	Household sector	12,943	13,806	13,844	13,611	13,386
4	Nonfarm corporate business	5,943	6,703	6,951	6,964	7,176
5	Nonfarm noncorporate business	3,196	3,650	3,972	3,672	3,475
6	Farm business	204	219	223	221	225
7	State and local governments	2,008	2,199	2,251	2,360	2,465
8	Federal government	4,885	5,122	6,362	7,805	9,386
9	**Rest of the world**	1,883	2,126	1,709	2,014	2,115
10	**Financial sectors**	14,291	16,217	17,123	15,618	14,171
11	Commercial banking	1,002	1,263	1,425	1,666	1,852
12	U.S.-chartered commercial banks	498	630	709	576	805
13	Foreign banking offices in the U.S.	0	1	0	0	0
14	Bank holding companies	503	633	717	1,090	1,047
15	Savings institutions	319	423	356	152	127
16	Credit unions	19	32	41	27	26
17	Life insurance companies	14	29	55	48	45
18	Government-sponsored enterprises	2,628	2,910	3,182	2,707	6,435
19	Agency- and GSE-backed mortgage pools	3,841	4,464	4,961	5,377	1,139
20	ABS issuers	4,199	4,544	4,135	3,350	2,353
21	Finance companies	1,144	1,280	1,200	1,044	962
22	REITs	411	421	373	339	350
23	Brokers and dealers	69	65	143	93	130
24	Funding corporations	645	786	1,253	817	751

Source: Federal Reserve Flow of Funds

the data series can be easily downloaded from 1945. Much of the analysis in this book is built on the data supplied in the *Flow of Funds* report.

The Rest of the World

The third development responsible for the credit conflagration in the United States originated outside the country. As can be seen in Exhibit 1.7, lenders from "the rest of the world" supplied 15 percent of all credit within the United States by 2007, a figure that came to roughly $7 trillion that year.

It is crucial to understand that this money, which was lent to the United States, originated on the printing presses of Asian central banks. It was newly created fiat money and a requisite part of Asia's export-led growth model. More than any other single factor, it was responsible for creating the global imbalances that destabilized the world.

Chapter 2 details how the creation of the equivalent of nearly $7 trillion in fiat money outside the United States between 1971 and 2007 exacerbated the extraordinary credit dynamic already underway inside the United States.

Notes

1. Irving Fisher, *The Purchasing Power of Money: Its Determination and Relation to Credit, Interest and Crises* (New York: The Macmillan Company, 1912), p. 131.
2. Council of Economic Advisers, 1968 Economic Report of the President, p. 16, http://fraser.stlouisfed.org/publications/ERP/issue/1162/download/5727/ERP_1968.pdf.
3. The Federal Reserve Act of 1913, p. 17, http://en.wikisource.org/wiki/Federal_Reserve_Act.
4. Joshua N. Feinman, "Reserve Requirements: History, Current Practice, and Potential Reform," Federal Reserve Bulletin, June 1993.
5. The Fed's website: Reserve Requirements, http://www.federalreserve.gov/monetarypolicy/reservereq.htm.

CHAPTER 2

The Global Money Glut

The balance of payments commands, the balance of trade obeys, and not the other way round.

—Eugen von Boehm-Bawerk[1]

When the Bretton Woods international monetary system broke down in 1971, something extraordinary began to happen. The central banks of some countries began printing fiat money and using it to buy the currencies of other countries. Before 1971, currencies were pegged either directly or indirectly to gold. Therefore, there was nothing to be gained by creating fiat money in order to buy any other country's currency. When the fixed exchange rate system ended with the collapse of the Bretton Woods system, however, that changed. Gradually, it became apparent that a country could gain an export advantage if its central bank created fiat money and used it to buy the currencies of its trading partners. Such intervention served to push up the value of the other currencies and depress the value of the currency being created, making the products of the currency-manipulating country more price competitive in the international marketplace.

Central banks accumulated approximately $6.7 trillion worth of foreign exchange between 1971 and 2007, when the global economic crisis began to take hold. (See Exhibit 2.1.) To do so, they created the equivalent of $6.7 trillion worth of their own fiat money. Approximately 75 percent of that money, roughly $5 trillion, went into the United States and, by 2007, supplied 10 percent of total credit market debt (TCMD) there. That flood of foreign capital threw fuel on the credit boom that was already underway there thanks to the elimination of the requirement that dollars be backed by gold and the near elimination of the requirement for the financial system to hold liquidity reserves. Thus, the creation of foreign fiat money and its investment into the United States was the third "financial innovation"

17

EXHIBIT 2.1 Total Foreign Exchange Reserves, 1948 to 2007

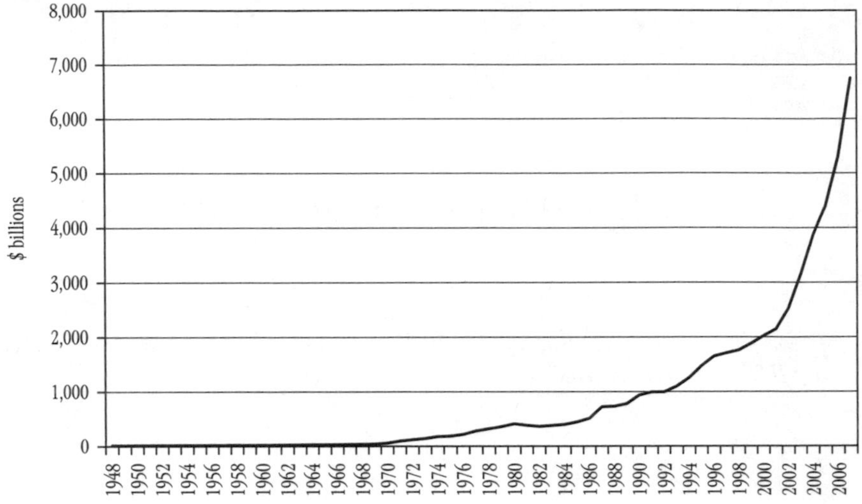

Source: IMF

responsible for the extraordinary proliferation of credit in the United States in recent decades.

Fed Chairman Ben Bernanke blamed the flood of foreign capital entering the country on a *global savings glut*. That is nonsense. The citizens of other countries did not save so much that they were unable to find profitable investment opportunities at home and therefore were compelled to invest in the United States, as Bernanke's theory suggests. The glut that inundated the United States was a glut of fiat money created by central bankers intent on manipulating their currency in order to boost their countries' exports.

This chapter explores how foreign fiat money creation on a mindboggling scale added to the credit inundations that wrecked havoc on the U.S. economy.

The Financial Account

Investment flows into and out of a country are recorded in the financial account of that country's balance of payments. A country that receives more investment from abroad than it makes abroad will have a surplus on its financial account. The United States has had a surplus on its financial account every year since 1983; and since the turn of the century that surplus has become extraordinarily large. This can be seen in Exhibit 2.2.

EXHIBIT 2.2 The U.S. Financial Account Balance, 1970 to 2007

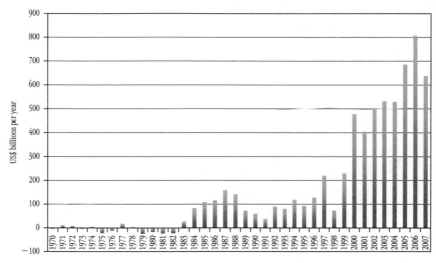

Source: IMF

An imbalance of investments on this scale was not possible under a gold standard. It would have involved the outflow of huge quantities of gold from the countries making the foreign investments. At a time when gold was money, the loss of so much gold would have caused a sharp contraction of the money supply and that would have created an economic crisis. In the post–Bretton Woods' world, however, where money can be created on demand and without limit, the constraint previously imposed by a finite amount of money is no longer a concern.

The investments that resulted in the extraordinary surplus on the U.S. financial account were funded with fiat money created by central banks outside the United States. This can be seen very clearly in Exhibit 2.3, which compares the annual increase in total foreign exchange reserves with the balance on the U.S. financial account.

From 1971 to 2007, total foreign exchange reserves increased by $6.7 trillion. Over the same period, the surplus on the U.S. financial account amounted to $6.3 trillion. The former funded the latter. Such a large surplus on the U.S. financial account could not have occurred had central banks outside the United States not created so much fiat money.

Alan Greenspan and Ben Bernanke have frequently attempted to explain the massive surplus on the U.S. financial account by blaming a global savings glut and by citing the overwhelming attractiveness of the U.S. financial markets relative to those elsewhere. The true explanation is that a dozen or so central banks have printed nearly $7 trillion worth of fiat money between 1971 and 2007 (and $3 trillion more subsequently) in order

EXHIBIT 2.3 The Annual Increase in Total Foreign Exchange Reserves vs. The U.S.
Financial Account Balance, 1970 to 2007

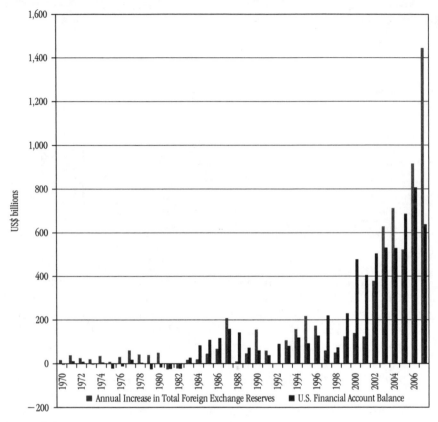

Source: IMF

to manipulate the value of their currencies so as to achieve strong export-led
growth.

Exhibit 2.4 lists the countries responsible.

How It Works

Exactly how do central banks create money and accumulate foreign exchange
reserves?

China has the largest amount of foreign exchange reserves. Therefore,
it will be used as the case study to illustrate how central banks accumulate
reserves. In 2007, China's trade surplus with the United States was $259
billion. In other words, China sold the United States $259 billion more in

EXHIBIT 2.4 Foreign Exchange Reserves
Top 15 Countries in 2007

US$ billions	2000	2007	Increase from 2000 to 2007
China	168	1,530	1,362
Japan	355	953	598
Russia	24	467	442
Saudi Arabia	20	305	286
Taiwan	107	270	164
India	38	267	229
Korea	96	262	166
Brazil	32	179	147
Singapore	80	163	83
Hong Kong	108	153	45
Algeria	12	110	98
Malaysia	28	101	73
Mexico	36	87	52
Thailand	32	85	53
Libya	12	79	67

Source: IMF

goods and services than the United States sold to China that year. When Chinese companies sell their goods in the United States, they are paid in dollars. In 2007, those companies took their surplus of $259 billion back to China. Most of those companies wanted to convert their U.S. dollars into Chinese yuan. However, had they bought $259 billion worth of yuan in the foreign exchange market without government intervention, the value of the yuan would have appreciated very sharply. The surge in the value of the currency would have made Chinese exports less competitive, which would have caused China's export growth and economic growth to slow.

A slowdown in growth was not part of the Chinese government's plan. Therefore, the government instructed the central bank, the People's Bank of China (PBOC), to buy all the dollars coming into China at a fixed exchange rate so that the yuan would not appreciate. And that is what the PBOC did. The central bank created the equivalent of $259 billion worth of fiat yuan and used it to buy $259 billion at a fixed exchange rate so that the yuan would not appreciate. The Chinese companies who brought the dollars into China were able to convert their dollars into yuan and then do with their yuan whatever they pleased. The PBOC, meanwhile, ended up with an addition $259 billion.

It must be understood that the PBOC acquired those dollars with fiat money it created from thin air specifically for that purpose. That is how central banks accumulate foreign exchange reserves, by creating fiat money and using it to purchase the currencies of other countries. Central banks have no means of obtaining large amounts of money other than by creating it.

Therefore, in order to have obtained the equivalent of $6.7 trillion in foreign exchange reserves by 2007, the central banks in possession of those reserves must have first created that much fiat money. Money creation on that scale was without precedent. That new money impacted the global economy with tremendous force. In fact, its impact was transformative. It underwrote globalization.

To complete this story, it is necessary to tie in the U.S. current account deficit. The current account primarily comprises a country's trade balance plus net transfer payments (such as foreign aid). The United States has had a very large trade and current account deficit for three decades. For every country, the balance on the current account is the mirror image of the balance on the financial account. That is because every country's balance of payment must balance, just as every family's books must balance. If a family spends more than it earns, it must borrow the difference to balance its books. So, too, must a country. A country that "invests" more than it "saves" will have a current account deficit, and it will have to borrow from abroad to pay for it. Thus, its financial account will show a surplus. (See Exhibit 2.5.)

In the past, when a country had a current account deficit, its currency would depreciate against other currencies. That made its exports cheaper on the global market and it made the products of other countries more expensive to import. Thus, there was an adjustment mechanism that worked to bring that country's trade back into balance. It doesn't work that way anymore.

Never before has a country incurred current account deficits on the enormous scale that the United States has experienced in recent years. The reason the dollar does not depreciate enough to correct the U.S. trade deficit is because many of the countries that the United States trades with are manipulating the currency's value by creating fiat money and buying dollars. The extent to which a country acts in this manner can be seen in the amount of foreign exchange that country's central bank holds. Thus the U.S. trade deficit and its financial account surplus are both the result of fiat money creation and currency manipulation by many of the United States' trading partners.

While fiat money created for this purpose is not solely responsible for bringing about the global economic crisis, it has been one of the leading culprits.

EXHIBIT 2.5 The U.S. Current Account vs. the U.S. Financial Account

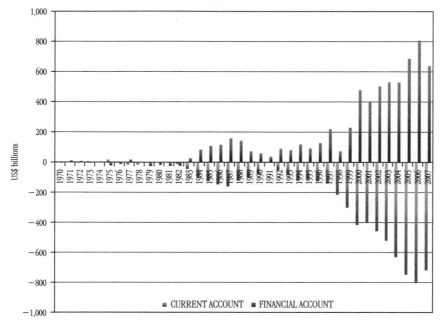

Source: IMF

What Percentage of Total Foreign Exchange Reserves Are Dollars?

Most countries disclose the breakdown of their foreign exchange reserves by currency. China, however, does not. Given that China holds more reserves than any other country (approximately a third of the total), the exact breakdown of the composition of total foreign exchange reserves cannot be determined.

Dollars made up 64 percent of the total reserves of those countries that did disclose in 2007. If China's reserves were included, that figure would most probably be much closer to 75 percent. China generally has a large trade surplus with the United States and a smaller trade deficit with much of the rest of the world. Therefore, it is likely that more than 80 percent of China's reserves are held in dollars.

Total foreign exchange reserves amounted to $6.7 trillion at the end of 2007. Of that sum, $5 trillion was held in dollars assuming the 75 percent ratio already suggested. Euros were the next largest component, making up an estimated 20 percent of the total or the equivalent of $1.3 trillion. Most of the remaining reserves were comprised of pounds and yen.[2]

What to Do with So Many Dollars?

As central banks accumulate foreign exchange reserves, whether in the form of dollars, Euros, pounds, or yen, they invest them in order to generate income. It is important to understand that they cannot invest reserves in their own economies without first converting the foreign currencies into the domestic currency. That, of course, would push up the value of the domestic currency and defeat the purpose of buying the reserves in the first place. So that is not an option.

The simplest course is to invest the foreign currency into investment vehicles denominated in that currency; and that is normally what is done. For instance, dollar reserves are invested in dollar-denominated bonds, euro reserves in euro-denominated bonds and so on. However, it is possible for the central bank holding the reserves to convert one currency into another and then to invest the money into investment vehicles denominated in the second currency. A central bank might wish to diversify its foreign reserve portfolio to reduce the weighting held in dollars, for example. However, the extent to which this actually does occur is limited for reasons both political and economic. If China used its dollar reserves to buy yen, for instance, it would push up the yen and damage Japan's exports. The Japanese government would protest and China would have to stop buying yen or else face retaliation from Japan. Therefore, relatively little diversification occurs.

That means the central banks accumulating foreign exchange reserves invested roughly $5 trillion in U.S. dollar–denominated assets and the equivalent of $1.3 trillion in euro-denominated assets between the breakdown of Bretton Woods and 2007, the year before crisis began. Most of the rest of this chapter will consider the impact that the investment of $5 trillion into dollar-denominated assets had on the U.S. credit market.

In 2007, TCMD outstanding in the United States amounted to $50 trillion. Therefore, the $5 trillion invested into the United States by foreign central banks accounted for 10 percent of all the credit extended in the country. Where did those central banks invest so much money?

Central banks are conservative. They prefer to invest in government bonds since they are believed to be the safest asset class. The U.S. government, however, simply did not issue enough bonds to satisfy $5 trillion worth of demand from foreign central banks. Exhibit 2.6 illustrates the large gap between the amount of dollars central banks outside the United States accumulated as foreign exchange reserves and the amount of bonds the U.S. government sold.

Note: In Exhibit 2.6, bond sales and buybacks are assumed to exactly match the government's budget deficits and surpluses each year. The figures for foreign exchange reserves are calculated by multiplying the actual increase

EXHIBIT 2.6 U.S. Government Debt Issuance (and Retirement) vs. the Increase in Dollar-denominated Foreign Exchange Reserves

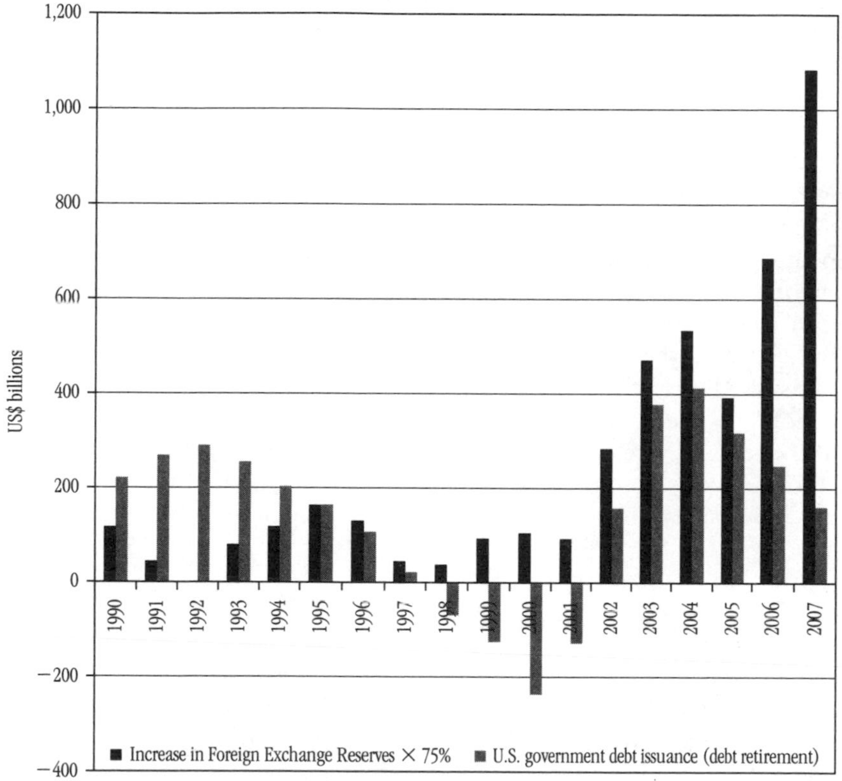

Source: IMF, Office of Management and Budget

in total foreign exchange reserves each year by 75 percent, since dollars are estimated to account for 75 percent of total reserves.

Notice that beginning in 1996, the increase in dollar reserves exceeded the amount of debt the U.S. government issued every year. Between 1996 and 2007, the government sold $1.25 trillion in new debt, while the cumulative increase in dollar reserves amounted to $3.96 trillion. In other words, the central banks accumulating those dollar reserves could have bought every new U.S. government bond sold between 1996 and 2007 and still had $2.7 trillion left over to invest in other dollar-denominated assets.

So, what did they actually do? The amount of government bonds bought by foreign central banks is public information. The Fed's Flow of Funds data reveal that "official" (i.e., government) buyers from the "rest of the world" (ROW) bought $1.13 trillion worth of U.S. government bonds between 1996 and 2007. That was equivalent to 90 percent of all new bonds the government sold during that period. However, they did not buy up 90 percent of the government bonds sold in each auction during those years. That is clear from the information released following every treasury auction. That means that central banks used the dollars they accumulated to buy a combination of new bonds at auction and older government bonds that had been sold in earlier years (i.e., both new bonds as they were sold by the government and older bonds already owned by other investors).

That explains a great deal about the behavior of U.S. interest rates during that period. When foreign central banks bought bonds that had been issued in earlier years, bonds then owned by other investors, they pushed up the price of those bonds and drove down their yields. That explains Chairman Greenspan's so-called "conundrum" over why government bond yields wouldn't rise despite the 17 rate hikes by the Fed between June 2004 and June 2006, which were designed to push them up. In other words, the Fed lost control over U.S. interest rates and, therefore, over the economy as the result of central banks outside the United States creating fiat money and investing it in U.S. government bonds. By the end of 2007, "official" investors from the ROW owned 34 percent of all U.S. government debt, up from 16 percent in 1996. (See Exhibit 2.7.)

What about the Remaining $2.8 Trillion?

The investment of $1.13 trillion into government bonds only absorbed 28 percent of the nearly $4 trillion in dollar reserves central banks accumulated between 1996 and 2007. Where was the other $2.8 trillion invested? Fannie Mae, Freddie Mac, and the other smaller government-sponsored enterprises (GSEs) absorbed $929 billion of it.

Over those 12 years, the GSEs issued and guaranteed nearly $5 trillion in debt. Of that amount, "official" buyers from the ROW bought 19 percent.[3] By the end of 2007, foreign official buyers owned 13 percent of all GSE and GSE-backed securities. Of course, when Fannie and Freddie issued debt, they used the proceeds to acquire mortgages. Thus, the official foreign buyers (composed almost entirely of central banks) were indirectly responsible for pumping $929 billion into the inflating U.S. property bubble.

With $1.13 trillion, official foreign buyers acquired the equivalent of 90 percent of all new governments bonds sold between 1996 and 2007; and with another $929 billion they acquired 19 percent of all the debt issued or backed by the GSEs over that period. What did they do with the remaining $1.94 trillion they are believed to have acquired as foreign exchange reserves? Those dollars may have been invested in U.S. corporate bonds or in U.S. equities. The *Flow of Funds* data do not disclose the stakes held by "official" buyers in U.S. corporate bonds and in U.S. equities.

EXHIBIT 2.7 The Rest of the World's Holdings of U.S. Securities 1996 Compared to 2007

| | 1996 | | | 2007 | | | |
	Total Outstanding US$ billions	ROW Holdings US$ billions	% of Total	Total Outstanding US$ billions	ROW Holdings US$ billions	ROW as % of Total %	Increase from 1996 US$ billions
Treasury securities (Govt.)	3,782	1,040	28%	5,122	2,376	46%	1,336
Official		**606**	**16%**		**1,737**	**34%**	**1,130**
Private		434	11%		640	12%	206
GSE & GSE-backed securities	2,609	134	5%	7,375	1,582	21%	1,448
Official		**25**	**1%**		**954**	**13%**	**929**
Private		110	4%		628	9%	518
U.S. corporate bonds	3,140	432	14%	11,435	2,719	24%	2,287
U.S. corporate equities	9,748	584	6%	25,576	2,812	11%	2,228

Source: Federal Reserve, *Flow of Funds Accounts of the United States*

Therefore, it is only possible to speculate. However, those dollars must have been invested in U.S. dollar-denominated assets and they must have put very considerable upward pressure on the prices of the assets in which they were invested.

Exhibit 2.7 compares the ROW's holding U.S. Treasury securities (government bonds), GSE debt, corporate bonds and equities in 1996 and 2007. It provides a breakdown between official investors (i.e., governments) and private investors for Treasury securities and GSE debt, but not for corporate bonds or equities. The increase in the share of U.S. assets held by foreign investors over this 12-year period is striking. The ROW's share of U.S. Treasury securities increased from 28 percent of the total in 1996 to 46 percent in 2007. The ROW's share in GSE debt rose from 5 percent to 21 percent; in corporate bonds from 14 percent to 24 percent; and in U.S. equities from 6 percent to 11 percent.

It is important to emphasize that much of the increase in the ROW's ownership of U.S. securities was the result of central banks creating fiat money, buying dollars, and investing those dollars in U.S. dollar-denominated assets. No other conclusion is possible.

Wherever that money was invested, it drove up asset prices, resulting in a significant impact on the U.S. economy. To the extent that it went into bonds, it drove up bond prices and drove down bond yields. That reduction in yields resulted in many investments being made that would not have been undertaken at a higher level of borrowing costs. To the extent that the dollars were invested in equities, they pushed up stock prices and created a wealth effect that permitted more consumption to occur than would have been possible otherwise. In short, those dollars distorted the U.S. economy by funding bad investments and excessive consumption, thus increasing its vulnerability to the downturn that got underway in late 2007.

Debunking the Global Savings Glut Theory

It is necessary here to set aside a few pages to discredit Ben Bernanke's global savings glut theory, which attributes the flood of foreign capital into the United States to the propensity of certain countries to "save" too much.

Traditionally, trade imbalances were understood to be caused by differences in national levels of saving and investment. National savings comprise the savings of the household sector, the business sector, and the government sector. Investment is made up primarily of investments in factories and equipment, as well as residential investment, the building of houses and apartment buildings. The rationale for attributing the trade imbalance to the difference in national levels of savings and investment runs as follows.

If a country invests more than it saves, then that country can borrow from abroad to finance that gap. In that case, that country would have a surplus on its financial account and (since the balance of payments must balance) a deficit on its current account. In other words, a country that invests more than it saves will have a current account deficit:

Investment > Savings = Current account deficit

Conversely, a country that saves more than it invests can lend its surplus savings to other countries. It then will have a financial account deficit (money flows abroad) and (again, since the balance of payments must balance) a current account surplus. Thus, a country that saves more than it invests will have a current account surplus:

Savings > Investment = Current account surplus

Fed Chairman Bernanke has often used this reasoning to explain the United States' massive current account deficit. Some countries such as China, he argues, save more than they invest, causing them to have a current account surplus and a glut of savings that they need to lend abroad to savings-deficient countries like the United States. This allows the United States to borrow from abroad and invest more than it saves, which produces the U.S. current account deficit.

Bernanke often used this argument to explain away the U.S. current account deficit, even as it grew to terrifying proportions. It peaked at $800 billion in 2006. Bernanke liked to explain that countries such as China, Japan, Korea, and Taiwan had such a high propensity to save that it simply wasn't possible for them to find profitable investment opportunities for so much savings in their own countries (despite the very high rates of economic growth that most of those countries experienced). Therefore, they were compelled to lend to the United States, thereby causing America's massive current account deficit. That line of reasoning became known as Bernanke's *global savings glut theory.*

That argument ignores one very important fact: Most of the money those countries invest in the United States is not derived from savings. The money those countries invest is newly created fiat money. When the PBOC created $460 billion worth of yuan in 2007 to manipulate its currency by buying dollars, that $460 billion worth of yuan was not "saved," it was created from thin air as part of government policy designed to hold down the value of its currency so as to perpetuate China's low-wage trade advantage. That is a very important difference. It introduces a third variable in addition to saving and investment, fiat money creation. Therefore, the equations expressing the determinants of the balance on the current account must be rewritten as follows:

(Savings + Fiat money creation) > Investment = Current account surplus

When a country's savings when combined with the paper money created by its central bank exceed the amount of its investment, then that country will have a current account surplus that will force other countries that do not create as much paper money to have current account deficits. And,

Investment > (Savings + Fiat money creation) = Current account deficit

Thus, it has not been a *savings* imbalance so much as an imbalance in the amount of paper money being created by the world's central banks that is responsible for the global imbalances that destabilized the world. Seen in this light, it is clear that the paper money creation by the PBOC and other currency manipulating central banks, which amounted to nearly $5 trillion between 1999 and 2007 alone, is responsible for destabilizing the world economy, and not differences in the rate of real "savings," as Bernanke contends.

China's economy has been growing at roughly 10 percent a year for two decades. It has the highest level of investment relative to GDP any country has ever experienced (46 percent in 2009). It is absurd to argue that there are not enough attractive investment opportunities in China to absorb its savings and that China therefore is compelled to lend its surplus savings to the United States. The truth is that China's central bank prints yuan and uses it to buy dollars in order to hold down the value of the yuan to support export-led growth. It is the dollars that the PBOC accumulates in that manner that are "lent" to the United States. The money China pumps into the United States drives up asset prices, drives down interest rates, and funds a wide range of malinvestment. In the years leading up to the crisis, it fueled a credit bubble that pacified the Americans who were losing their manufacturing jobs to low-wage Chinese competitors.

Think of the Federal Reserve's actions since 2008. In two rounds of quantitative easing, the Fed created $2.3 trillion. That money is now on the Fed's balance sheet. It is considered to be part of the U.S. "monetary authority's" assets. Is it savings? Did the Fed "save" $2.3 trillion? Of course not. It "printed" that money. That is exactly what the People's Bank of China, the Bank of Japan, the Bank of Korea, the Central Bank of the

Republic of China (Taiwan), and a long list of other central banks have been doing for many years. There has been a glut; of that there can be no doubt. But it has been a paper money printing glut, not a savings glut. Savers should not be blamed for saving the money they have earned. Central banks are to blame and should be held accountable for printing money, manipulating their currencies, and destabilizing the global economy. The paper money they have created has played a leading role in bringing the world economy to the brink of catastrophe.

The extent to which the U.S. government has been complicit in this arrangement is uncertain. There can be no question, however, that the government found it easier to finance its massive budget deficits as a result of those inflows. There can also be no doubt that this arrangement is responsible for the hollowing out of the U.S. manufacturing base, the current high rates of U.S. unemployment, and the unprecedented duration of joblessness among those who are unemployed.

Will China Dump Its Dollars?

Many fear that China will stop buying debt from the United States or that it will suddenly dump the U.S. debt it already owns. It won't. If China stopped buying U.S. debt, its economy would collapse because that would mean that it had stopped manipulating its currency by buying dollars. In that case, its currency would soon double in value and then double again relative to the U.S. dollar as Chinese exporters converted their large export earnings into yuan. That would be more than enough to pop the great Chinese bubble.

As for China selling the $2.5 trillion worth of dollar-denominated assets it is estimated to hold among its foreign exchange reserves—even assuming they could find buyers for that many dollars—where would China invest the $2.5 trillion worth of proceeds? There are not $2.5 trillion worth of euro- or yen- or pound-denominated credit instruments that they could buy. Even the attempt to move a few hundred billion dollars into any other currency would drive up that currency so sharply that the country issuing that currency would insist China stop or face retaliatory consequences. And, if the PBOC converted even as much as $500 billion into yuan, it would be the equivalent of a currency rocket launch that would send the yuan to the moon.

So, the bottom line is this: Not only can China not sell the dollar reserves it now owns; it must continue accumulating more dollar reserves each year in line with its massive trade surplus with the United States. Otherwise, the enormous amount of dollars its exporters earn in the United States each year will push up the yuan when the exporters bring them back home to China and convert them into yuan. That is something the Chinese authorities cannot allow because a much higher yuan would be sure to throw China's economy into crisis.

Notes

1. Joseph Schumpeter, *Ten Great Economists, from Marx to Keynes* (New York: Oxford University Press, 1951).
2. These estimates were reached using information published by the IMF on disclosed and undisclosed reserves.
3. Fed's *Flow of Funds Account of the United States, second quarter 2011* (see Exhibit 2.7, Rest of the World).

CHAPTER 3

Creditopia

The only cause of depression is prosperity.

—Clement Juglar[1]

W hat did a $50 trillion expansion of credit do to the U.S. economy? First, it brought about unprecedented prosperity in the United States by creating wealth, profits, jobs, and abundant tax revenues. Moreover, it generated a vast amount of financial capital. But $50 trillion of credit did more than make the United States prosperous; it fundamentally transformed the structure of its economy. It caused the focus of economic activity to shift from producing goods to providing services, and, finally, to speculation. By the beginning of the twenty-first century, easy credit had created a world in which all that was necessary to become rich was to borrow money and buy assets. It was a utopia for investors—a Creditopia.

This chapter describes that economic transformation. It begins with a look at who borrowed the money.

Who Borrowed the Money?

At the end of World War II, the U.S. government was by far the country's largest debtor. In 1945, the government owed 71 percent of all the debt outstanding in the country. The corporate sector came next with 13 percent, followed by the household sector with 8 percent. The financial sector owed only 1 percent of all debt. (See Exhibit 3.1.)

By 2007, the relative share of indebtedness of these sectors had changed radically. By then, U.S. government debt had declined to 10 percent of total credit market debt outstanding. That was a very large relative decline, but not surprising. It is natural that government debt would decline from a very high level during the decades following a major war. There was no

EXHIBIT 3.1 Total Credit Market Debt Owed

	1945	2007
TCMD $ billions percent of total:	355	50,043
Federal government	71%	10%
Household sector	8%	28%
Corporate sector	13%	13%
Noncorporate businesses	1%	7%
Financial sector including:	1%	32%
Commercial banks	0%	3%
GSEs & GSE-backed mortgage pools	0%	15%
Issuers of asset-backed securities	0%	9%
Miscellaneous	6%	10%
	100%	100%

Source: Federal Reserve, *Flow of Funds Accounts of the United States, second quarter 2011*

change in the corporate sector's share of debt. It had remained unchanged at 13 percent.

The noteworthy and critical developments came in the household sector and the financial sector. The household sector's share of debt had surged by 20 percentage points to 28 percent, while the financial sector had become the biggest borrower of all, with 32 percent of all debt. The sharp jump in the level of debt of those two sectors was surprising. What had happened?

Consider first the financial sector. In the late 1940s, the financial sector issued hardly any debt at all. Deposits supplied almost all of the sector's funding. That began to change during the 1960s.

As Exhibit 3.2 shows, of the five most heavily indebted sectors, the financial sector had the lowest absolute level of debt until 1966, when it overtook the noncorporate business sector. In 1988, it pulled ahead of the federal government to become the third heaviest indebted sector. Two years later, the indebtedness of the financial sector surpassed that of the corporate sector. And, in 1998, the financial sector moved into first place, having borrowed more even than the household sector. By 2007, the financial sector was $16 trillion in debt. The household sector owed $14 trillion. The corporate sector ranked a distant third with $7 trillion. The federal government owed $5 trillion and the noncorporate business sector owed $4 trillion.

That was a monumental change in the structure of the U.S. credit markets. Traditionally, the financial sector had acted only as an intermediary

EXHIBIT 3.2 Who Owes The Debt?

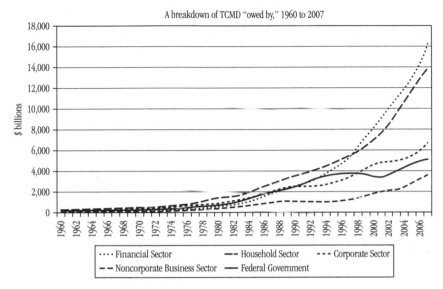

Source: Federal Reserve, *Flow of Funds Accounts of the United States, second quarter 2011*

between savers and borrowers, accepting deposits and making loans. By the end of the century, however, the financial sector itself had become the country's largest borrower. Fannie Mae and Freddie Mac were the principal agents behind that change.

Fannie and Freddie had never been deposit-taking institutions. They traditionally raised funds by issuing bonds. As government-sponsored enterprises (GSEs), they could raise money cheaply because investors believed their bonds were implicitly backed by the U.S. government. Fannie and Freddie used the funds they raised to buy mortgages from banks and other mortgage originators. They retained some of those mortgages on their books as assets. Most, however, they resold to other investors—but they resold them with a performance guarantee attached. In that way, Fannie and Freddie earned an additional fee for guaranteeing that the mortgages they sold would meet their interest and principal payments on schedule.

Entities known as "agency- and GSE-backed mortgage pools" (essentially special-purpose vehicles) bought most of the mortgages sold and guaranteed by Fannie and Freddie. They, too, raised funds by issuing debt. By the end of 2007, the GSEs had $2.9 trillion in debt outstanding, while the agency- and GSE-backed mortgage pools were $4.5 trillion in debt.

It was eventually disclosed that Fannie and Freddie themselves were the "beneficial owners" of most of the agency- and GSE-backed mortgage

EXHIBIT 3.3 Who Borrowed the Money within the Financial Sector?

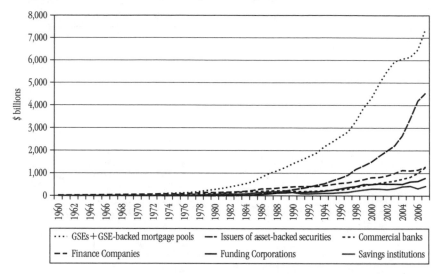

Source: Federal Reserve, *Flow of Funds Accounts of the United States, second quarter 2011*

pools. That came to light after they were taken over by the government and put into in *conservatorship.* In other words, most of the agency- and GSE-backed mortgage pools were essentially subsidiaries of the GSEs. As a result, beginning in 2010, most of the assets and liabilities of those mortgage pools were consolidated onto the GSEs' balance sheets. Exhibit 3.3 shows the extraordinary expansion of GSE debt.

The combined debt of the GSEs and agency- and GSE-backed mort-gage pools first hit $1 trillion in 1988. By 1994, it had doubled to $2 trillion. After six more years it had reached $4 trillion. And, by 2008, just before they were taken over by the government, their debt had doubled yet again to $8 trillion. That was an eightfold increase in debt over 20 years. It is also worth noting that foreign "official" investors, principally central banks, bought nearly $1 trillion out of the $8 trillion in debt issued and guaranteed by the GSEs. Most of those purchases were funded through fiat money creation, as described in Chapter 2.

The second important change in the financial sector began during the 1990s when private-sector issuers of asset-backed securities began to repli-cate the business model of the GSEs. They issued debt and bought up assets such as traditional mortgages, subprime mortgages, credit card receivables, and student loans. They then combined, repackaged, and resold those assets to other investors in tranches with varying degrees of risk. Although they started later and even though the government clearly did not back their debt, they still managed to increase their indebtedness eightfold to $4.5 trillion in only 13 years.

By the time the credit crisis began in 2007, the debt issued (and the credit extended) by the GSEs and the asset-backed security (ABS) issuers had radically altered the size and structure of the U.S. economy. Combined, the GSEs and ABS issuers had $12 trillion in debt outstanding, up from $1 trillion 20 years earlier. To put that into perspective, consider that over the preceding 70 years, the U.S. government had fought World War II, the Korean War, the Cold War, the Vietnam War, and two Gulf Wars, had carried out numerous social welfare programs, and had sent a man to the moon, but had accumulated only a total of $5 trillion in debt in the process.

What did Fannie and Freddie and the ABS issuers do with all the money they borrowed? They lent it to the household sector in the form of mortgages and consumer credit. Between 1982 and 2007, the mortgage debt of the household sector rose ten times to $10.5 trillion. Consumer credit increased six times over the same period to $2.5 trillion. (See Exhibit 3.4.)

Relative to the overall size of the economy, the financial sector's debt rose from 21 percent of GDP in 1980 to 116 percent in 2007. The household sectors' debt rose from 50 percent to 98 percent of GDP over the same period. (See Exhibit 3.5.)

EXHIBIT 3.4 Home Mortgages and Consumer Credit

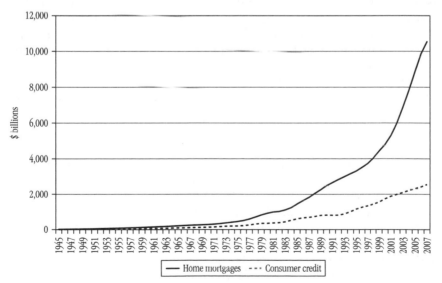

Source: Federal Reserve, *Flow of Funds Accounts of the United States, second quarter 2011*

EXHIBIT 3.5 Household and Financial Sector Debt to GDP

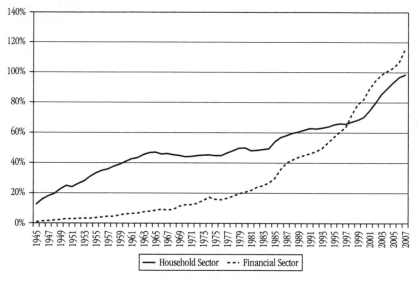

Source: Federal Reserve, *Flow of Funds Accounts of the United States, second quarter 2011*

Impact on the Economy

Adding all sectors together, total credit market debt averaged around 150 percent of GDP between 1946 and 1970. That ratio moved up gradually to 170 percent by the end of the 1970s, but then accelerated sharply during the 1980s, ending that decade at 230 percent. The rate of debt expansion slowed during most of the 1990s, but surged again from 1998. By 2007, total credit market debt to GDP had hit 360 percent. (See Exhibit 3.6.)

That sharp rise in the ratio of total debt to GDP denotes the extraordinary expansion of leverage in the economy, but, by itself, does not adequately capture the full extent of what had taken place. That ratio understates the impact that so much credit growth had on the economy. That is because credit, as it expanded, caused the economy to expand, too. The numerator in the equation influenced the denominator. Put differently, the credit growth caused the economic growth— or, at least, much of the economic growth.

It is easy to understand how rapid credit growth facilitates economic growth. When credit is expanding, consumers can borrow and spend more and businesses can borrow and invest more. Increasing consumption and investment create jobs and boost income and profits. Moreover, the expansion of credit tends to cause the price of assets such as stocks and property to increase, thereby pushing up the net worth of the public.

EXHIBIT 3.6 Total Credit Market Debt to GDP, 1946 to 2007

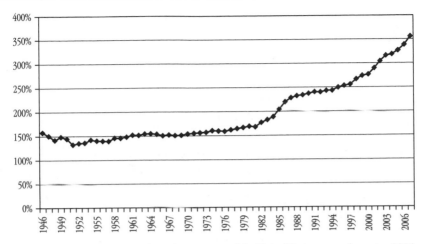

Source: Federal Reserve, *Flow of Funds Accounts of the United States, second quarter 2011*

Rising asset prices give the owners of assets more wealth, which they can use as collateral to borrow still more. This cycle of expanding credit leading to increased spending, investment, job creation and wealth, followed by still more borrowing, produces a happy upward spiral of prosperity—so long as it continues.

Net Worth

Exhibit 3.7 shows the increase in total credit market debt and in household net worth. They both moved sharply higher together. That is not a coincidence. As credit expanded, it drove up asset prices in the United States and created wealth.

The household sector's assets are composed of real estate (32 percent of the total), equities (25 percent), deposits (9 percent), directly held credit market instruments such as government and corporate bonds (5 percent), and miscellaneous other assets held in pension and retirement funds.

As credit expanded, it pushed up the value of most of those assets, thereby creating more wealth for the household sector. The great bull market in equities drove the Dow Jones Industrial Average up from 1,000 in 1982 to 14,000 in 2007. (See Exhibit 3.8.) Property prices also surged higher. As shown in Exhibit 3.9, the median price of a single family home rose from $64,000 in 1980 to $257,000 in 2007.

Higher asset prices not only created wealth, they also created a wealth effect that boosted spending. As individuals saw the value of their homes,

EXHIBIT 3.7 Household Net Worth and Total Credit Market Debt

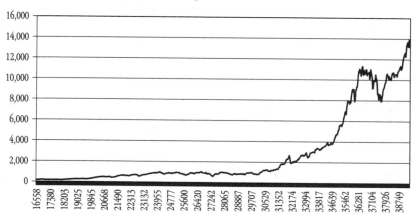

Source: Federal Reserve, *Flow of Funds Accounts of the United States, second quarter 2011*

EXHIBIT 3.8 Dow Jones Industrial Average

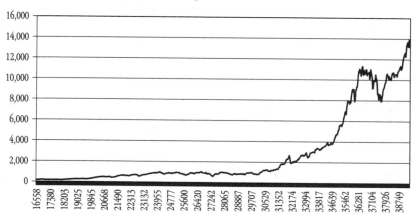

Source: Dow Jones & Company

equity portfolios, and retirement funds move sharply higher, they felt wealthier and they spent more. As home prices increased, many Americans raised cash by refinancing and extracting equity from their homes. The money they extracted, they spent. Consumption makes up 70 percent of U.S. GDP. From the mid-1990s, home equity extraction was the fuel that powered a great deal of that consumption.

EXHIBIT 3.9 Median Sales Price of Houses Sold

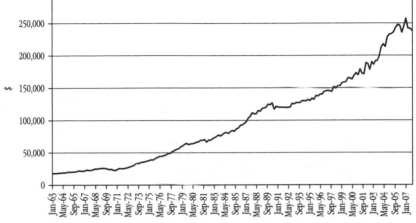

Source: U.S. Department of Commerce

Profits

The surge in debt, asset prices, and spending generated strong growth in profits. As total credit market debt doubled between 1999 and 2007, so did profits—for both the financial sector and the nonfinancial sector. (See Exhibit 3.10.)

Tax Revenue

Higher income and higher profits produced higher tax revenues for all levels of government. Federal tax revenues increased five times between 1980 and 2007. State and local tax revenues rose three times between 1988 and 2007. The surge in tax revenues made possible an even greater increase in government spending, which, in turn, created still more economic growth. (See Exhibit 3.11.)

Different, Not Just More

Credit did more to the U.S. economy than make it grow. It also radically changed its composition. Exhibit 3.12 shows the change in valued added by industry as a percentage of GDP from 1947 to 2007. First notice that the manufacturing sector, which had contributed more than a quarter

EXHIBIT 3.10 The Profits of the Nonfinancial Sector and the Financial Sector

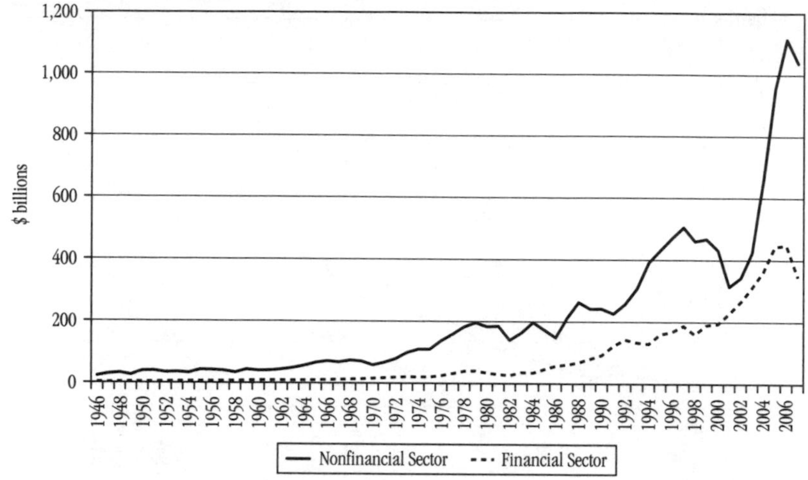

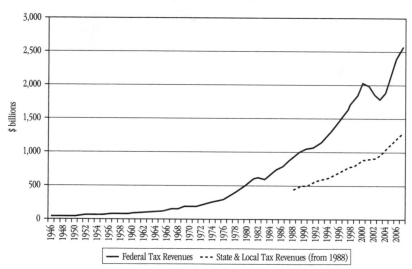

Source: Bureau of Economic Analysis

EXHIBIT 3.11 Tax Revenues: Federal, and State and Local

Source: Office of Management and Budget, Bureau of Economic Analysis

of all economic output during the first two decades after the war, went into steep decline just as the Bretton Woods System broke down in 1971. Afterward, the United States discovered it could buy its manufactured products from lower-cost producers abroad and pay for them with credit.

EXHIBIT 3.12 Value Added by Industry as Percentage of GDP

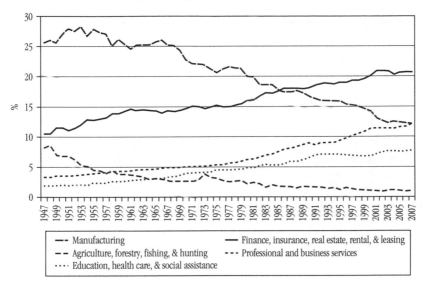

Source: Bureau of Economic Analysis

Consequently, the country's current account deficit blew out to extraordinary levels, peaking at $800 billion in 2006. By then, the manufacturing sector's contribution to GDP had declined to only 12 percent.

Meanwhile, the share of economic output of the finance and real estate sector grew, particularly after the credit boom of the early 1980s got underway. In 1986, the finance, insurance, real estate, rental, and leasing category (FIRE, for short) overtook manufacturing as the largest sector of the economy. Thanks to the credit-induced bubbles in the stock market and the property market, that sector eventually grew to account for more than a fifth of the country's economic output.

The professional and business services sector also grew notably, increasing its share of economic output from 6 percent in 1980 to 12 percent in 2007. That sector was composed largely of the law firms, accounting agencies, and rating agencies that all expanded their operations to cater to the increasingly complex needs of the financial industry. Finally, the share of economic value added contributed by education, health care, and social assistance also grew significantly, from less than 2 percent in 1947 to 8 percent in 2007. Government spending drove much of the growth in those areas. (See Exhibit 3.13.)

The trends in economic output were mirrored in the labor market. As illustrated in Exhibit 3.14, there were actually fewer jobs in the manufacturing sector in 2007 than there were in 1948, 14 million vs. 14.7 million. The service sector provided 67 percent of all jobs by 2007. Employment

EXHIBIT 3.13 Value Added by Industry as a Percentage of Gross Domestic Product
[Percent]

	1947	1948	2006	2007
Gross domestic product	100	100	100	100
Private industries	88	89	88	88
Agriculture, forestry, fishing, and hunting	8	9	1	1
Mining	2	3	2	2
Utilities	1	1	2	2
Construction	4	4	5	5
Manufacturing	26	26	12	12
Wholesale trade	6	6	6	6
Retail trade	10	9	7	6
Transportation and warehousing	6	6	3	3
Information	3	3	4	5
Finance, insurance, real estate, rental, and leasing	11	11	21	21
Professional and business services	3	3	12	12
Educational services, health care, and social assistance	2	2	8	8
Arts, entertainment, recreation, accommodation, & food services	3	3	4	4
Other services, except government	3	3	3	3
Government	13	11	12	13
Federal	8	7	4	4
State and local	4	4	9	9

Source: Bureau of Economic Analysis

expanded most significantly in the education, health care, and social assistance sector and in professional and business services. Those two categories were the second and third largest employers in absolute terms in 2007, with 18.5 million and 18.0 million workers, respectively. State and local government employed 19.4 million people, making that sector the country's largest overall employer.

By 2007, the service sector and the government sector had come to dominate the economy, both having been fueled by the direct and indirect impact of $50 trillion in credit growth.

In summary, that explosion of credit profoundly altered the nature of the economic activity in the United States. The business model of the country changed. As a portion of total output, the economy produced

EXHIBIT 3.14 Jobs: The Change in Employment by Sector, 2007 vs. 1948

(Thousands)	1948	1948	2007	2007	Change (thousands)	Change (percentage points)
Manufacturing	14,741	28.7%	13,883	9.7%	–858	–19.1%
Retail trade	4,785	9.3%	15,761	11.0%	10,976	1.6%
Federal	4,007	7.8%	5,091	3.5%	1,084	–4.3%
State and local	3,887	7.6%	19,424	13.5%	15,537	5.9%
Arts, entertainment, recreation, accommodation, & food services	2,548	5.0%	13,524	9.4%	10,976	4.4%
Wholesale trade	2,395	4.7%	6,049	4.2%	3,654	–0.5%
Construction	2,329	4.5%	7,893	5.5%	5,564	1.0%
Finance, insurance, real estate, rental, & leasing	1,790	3.5%	8,382	5.8%	6,592	2.3%
Professional & business services	1,712	3.3%	18,052	12.6%	16,340	9.2%
Education, health care, & social assistance	1,448	2.8%	18,538	12.9%	17,090	10.1%

Source: Bureau of Economic Analysis

far fewer goods, but provided far more services. Credit allowed America to buy all the manufactured goods it desired from abroad and credit financed the procurement of services at home. It could be argued that credit creation became the country's most important industry and debt its principal export.

Economic progress was no longer achieved the old-fashioned way through savings and investments, but, rather, by borrowing and consumption. That profound change was reflected in the sharp decline in the national savings rate, which dropped from 12 percent of national income in 1950 to 1.7 percent in 2007, as shown in Exhibit 3.15. On a net basis, a country cannot borrow and save at the same time. The United Stated chose to borrow.

Impact on Capital

Finally, consider the impact that the creation of $50 trillion in credit had on the capital structure of the financial system.

EXHIBIT 3.15 National Net Saving as a Percentage of Gross National Income, 1950 to 2007

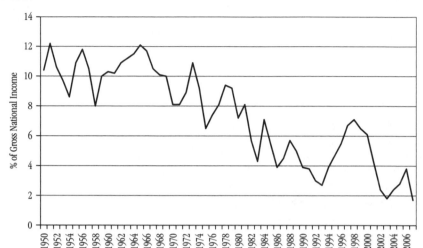

Source: Bureau of Economic Analysis

Credit and debt are two sides of the same coin. One person's debt is another person's asset. Therefore, the $50 trillion expansion of credit meant a $50 trillion expansion of both debt and assets. Over time, the quality of both deteriorated markedly as the leverage in the country grew and lending standards weakened. *Bank capital* is simply a bookkeeping entry that represents the difference between the banks' assets (composed of the debt owed by individuals, businesses, and other financial institutions) and their liabilities (composed of their own debt and the deposit they have accepted). Therefore, as the credit quality of their assets deteriorated, so too did the quality of their capital.

With each year that passed, the gap between the amount of debt outstanding relative to the size of the economy grew wider. Therefore, it became increasingly difficult for the economy to generate enough output and profitability to service the interest on that debt. As long as credit continued to expand rapidly and asset prices continued to inflate, debtors could easily refinance their assets and, in that way, raise enough cash to pay interest on their debt. When housing prices stopped inflating in 2007, however, no additional equity could be extracted and the defaults began. By that stage there was three-and-a-half times as much debt as economic output. (See Exhibit 3.16.)

When debtors default, the assets of the creditors are destroyed. During normal business conditions, the amount of debt in default is small and has

EXHIBIT 3.16 Total Credit Market Debt vs. GDP

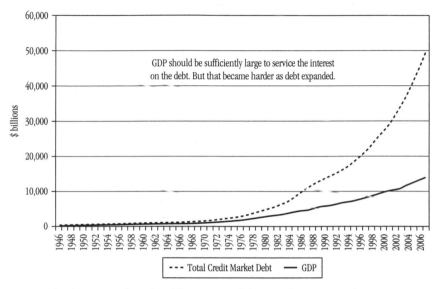

GDP should be sufficiently large to service the interest on the debt. But that became harder as debt expanded.

--- Total Credit Market Debt   — GDP

Source: Federal Reserve, *Flow of Funds Accounts of the United States, second quarter 2011*

no significant impact on the overall credit system. Now, however, following an extraordinary four-decade credit boom, it is not certain how much of the $50 trillion in debt can be serviced in the absence of additional credit expansion. That will depend on how much of that $50 trillion was invested in projects that can generate sufficient returns to meet the scheduled interest and principal repayments and how much was not. It is clear that a large amount of that debt cannot be repaid and will have to be written off, destroying the assets of the corresponding creditors. There is a real danger that the amount of bad debt is so large that it will destroy all the capital of the banking system.

The collapse of the investment banking industry very nearly caused a systemic collapse in 2008. Going into the crisis, the five largest U.S. investment banks had an extraordinary degree of leverage, ranging from 26 to 33 times (as measured by the ratio of total assets to equity and illustrated in Exhibit 3.17).

Those numbers do not capture the full extent of the risk to which those companies were exposed, however. For example, in 2007 Goldman Sachs had $42.8 billion in shareholders' equity and $1,120 billion in assets. In other words, its leverage was 26 times. In addition to that, the firm was exposed to trillions of dollars in derivatives positions, as measured by the notional value of the derivatives contracts. The notional value generally

EXHIBIT 3.17 Investment Banks Leverage

Ratio: Total Assets to Equity (X)	2003	2004	2005	2006	2007
Goldman Sachs	19	21	25	23	26
Lehman Brothers Holdings	24	24	24	26	31
Morgan Stanley	24	27	31	32	33
Merrill Lynch	17	20	19	22	32
Bear Stearns	28	28	27	29	n.a.

Sources: Annual Reports

greatly overstates the true risk inherent in those contracts so long as the counterparties to the trades do not default. In 2007, however, AIG was one of Goldman Sachs' major derivatives counterparties. So was Lehman Brothers. In 2008, Lehman Brothers defaulted. In all likelihood, AIG and most of the firm's other derivatives counterparties would have failed that year, too, had the U.S. government not intervened though the Treasury and the Fed to bail them out. Seen in that light, Goldman's $42.8 billion in capital could have evaporated in the blink of an eye.

When Lehman Brothers failed and Goldman's liquidity dried up in September 2008, the investment bank converted itself into a bank holding company overnight so that it could borrow money from the central bank. Morgan Stanley followed suit. Goldman Sachs and Morgan Stanley survived as bank holding companies. Merrill Lynch was acquired by Bank of America. Bear Stearns had already disappeared as the result of a government-assisted rescue and takeover by JP Morgan earlier in the year.

Lehman's inability to repay its debt destroyed a great deal of capital. Its default revealed just how poor the quality of much of the financial system's capital actually is.

There is a limit to how much debt an economy can bear. That limit is determined by the economy's ability to generate sufficient income to service the debt. Exhibit 3.18 helps put the relationship between credit and the economy into perspective. It shows the ratio of economic output (i.e., GDP) to total credit market debt in the United States. That ratio represents the return on credit. The sharp decline in the return on credit indicates that in recent decades, the economy has generated steadily less output per dollar borrowed. In other words, there has been a sharp decline in the marginal efficiency of credit. That decline reflects the extraordinary malinvestment that has occurred during the last three decades in particular. It also raises uncomfortable questions about how much more of the financial sector's capital will be destroyed during the years ahead.

EXHIBIT 3.18 The Ratio of GDP to Total Credit Market Debt

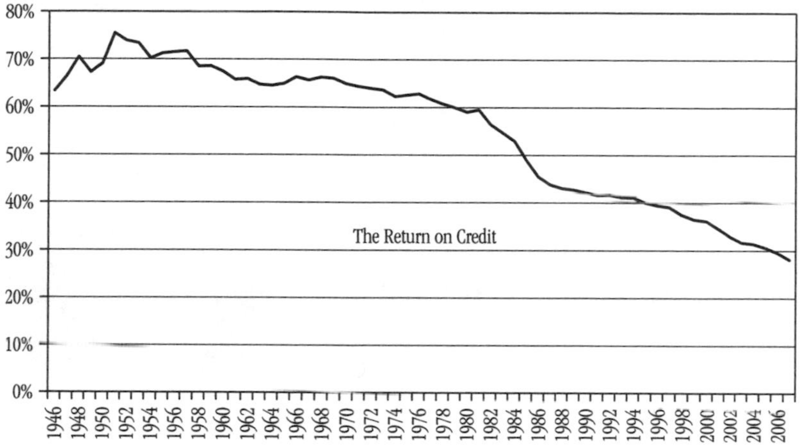

Source: Federal Reserve, Flow of Funds

Conclusion

The U.S. credit market can be thought of as an inverted pyramid. Back in 1968, an edifice composed of $1.3 trillion in credit balanced on a small foundation of gold valued at $10 billion. Then in March that year, Congress changed the law so that dollars no longer had to be backed by gold. Over the decades that followed, no more gold was added to the base, but another $50 trillion of credit was piled on top. In 2008, with nothing real to underpin it, the entire debt superstructure began to collapse upon itself. Credit had inflated the capital of the financial system, but when the credit blew up, the capital deflated and disappeared. There were no liquidity reserves to speak of. In the end, the Fed had to print $1.7 trillion of liquidity (QE round 1) to rescue the sector. Had the Fed not intervened, the financial system would not have survived. Only a relatively small amount of losses would have destroyed all the dubious capital depicted on the financial sector's balance sheet.

The nature of money changed in 1968, and that change transformed the economy. It has become increasingly difficult to distinguish between money and credit. Moreover, the amount of credit has grown so large relative to the amount of what was previously understood to be money that it has made money irrelevant. The new reality is that credit has displaced money as the key economic variable. That change is the subject of Chapter 4.

Note

1. Joseph Schumpeter, *History of Economic Analysis* (New York: Oxford University Press, 1954), p. 1123.

CHAPTER 4

The Quantity Theory of Credit

A credit-expansion boom must unavoidably lead to a process which everyday speech calls the depression.

—Ludwig von Mises[1]

So long as gold was money, credit creation was limited by the supply of gold. When the United States severed the link between dollars and gold in 1968, it removed all constraints on how much credit could be created. Over the following four decades, credit grew fiftyfold and transformed the economy both in size and structure.

Meanwhile, however, although the nature of money had changed, economic theory on the subject of money did not. For centuries, economists have understood that changes in the quantity of money affect the price level and, at least temporarily, the level of economic activity. That concept is known as the *quantity theory of money* and it is the foundation upon which *monetarism* and modern monetary policy was built.

In recent decades, the usefulness of the quantity theory of money as a tool for analyzing changes in the economy has broken down because the extraordinary expansion of credit has made money irrelevant in comparison. The money supply is no longer the most important factor affecting economic change. It is the credit supply that matters now. Consequently, the quantity theory of money must be adjusted to reflect that fact.

This chapter introduces the *quantity theory of credit,* which revises the quantity theory of money in a way that makes it applicable to the fiat money based economic system that has evolved since 1968. Focusing on credit instead of money, the quantity theory of credit creates a powerful analytical framework that explains the causes of the New Depression, as well as the government's policy response to it thus far. Even more importantly, it clarifies the probable course of future events since it can be used as a model to forecast economic growth (or contraction) based on assumptions about future credit growth. Therefore, it can be used to judge the potential effectiveness of proposed government policies, as well as the consequences for the economy should the government fail to act. In short, it is an invaluable tool for analyzing every aspect—past, present, and future—of the New Depression.

This chapter begins by explaining the quantity theory of money. It then describes the developments that transformed money and credit, making a revision of the quantity theory of money necessary. Finally, it explains the quantity theory of credit and how it differs from the quantity theory of money. By the end of this chapter, the disturbing implications of this theory will have become clear.

The Quantity Theory of Money

The quantity theory of money asserts that changes in the quantity of money in an economy cause a proportional change in the price level. The theory is centuries old. In his magisterial work *History of Economic Analysis*, Joseph Schumpeter credits Jean Bodin, a French political philosopher, for being the first to propound the theory in 1568. David Hume, John Stuart Mill, Ludwig von Mises (with a few qualifications), and Milton Friedman—along with many others—all accepted and wrote about the quantity theory.

In 1912, Irving Fisher published the definitive work on the subject, *The Purchasing Power of Money: Its Determination and Relation to Credit, Interest and Crises*.[2]

In that book, Fisher employed what he called *the equation of exchange* to demonstrate the relationship between the quantity of money and the price level. He expressed the equation of exchange as:

$$MV = PT$$

where:

M = Money (the average amount of money in circulation in the
    community during the year)
V = Velocity (the average rate of turnover of money)
P = Price level (the weighted average of all prices)
T = Trade (the volume of trade)

The statement $MV = PT$ must always be true, given the preceding definitions for M, V, P, and T. Essentially, it means the amount spent (MV)

is always equal to price of all the things bought (*PT*) for any particular community during any given period of time. *MV* is the quantity of money (*M*) multiplied by the number of times that money is used during the period (*V*). *PT* represents the price (*P*) of each product multiplied by the quantity purchased or the volume of trade (*T*).

The equation of exchange has been called an identity or a tautology. Schumpeter described it as an equilibrium condition. Fisher explained it as follows:

> *In each sale and purchase, the money and goods exchanged are ipso facto equivalent; for instance, the money paid for sugar is equivalent to the sugar bought. And in the grand total of all exchanges for a year, the total money paid is equal in value to the total value of the goods bought. The equation thus has a money side (the left side of the equation) and a goods side (the right side of the equation). The money side is the total money paid, and may be considered as the product of the quantity of money multiplied by its rapidity of circulation. The goods side is made up of the products of quantities of goods exchanged multiplied by their respective prices.*[3]

It is important to point out that the right side of the equation, *PT*, is equivalent to total economic output. It represents the price level multiplied by the volume of trade, or, in other words, the value of everything produced and sold by a community during a certain period of time. The value of all goods produced and sold by a country during one year is that country's gross domestic product, or GDP. Therefore,

$$MV = PT = GDP$$

The quantity theory of money holds—and Fisher demonstrated—that over the long run, changes in *M* cause a proportionate and lasting change in the price level (*P*) but have no impact on the velocity of money (*V*) and only a temporary impact on the volume of trade (*T*). Fisher reasoned that the velocity of money, its rate of turnover, depends on "individual habits" and "technical conditions" and has no discoverable relationship with the quantity of money. "It will depend on density of population, commercial customs, rapidity of transport, and other technical conditions, but not on the quantity of money," he wrote.[4]

He also explained that the impact of a change in the quantity of money on the volume of trade (*T*) only lasts during a transition period. He described the dynamics of the transition period as follows. An initial increase in the quantity of money (M) causes the price of goods sold by the business community to increase more quickly than the rate of interest they are required to pay to finance the production of those goods. That results in higher profits for businessmen. The improvement in profits prompts businesses to borrow and invest more, thus producing a pickup in the volume of trade (T). Sooner or later, however, interest rates begin to increase due to rising inflation. Eventually, interest rates catch up with the increase in prices, thereby causing profit margins to contract again. At that point, the business community realizes it has been too optimistic about profits. Consequently, businesses stop borrowing and investing, so the volume of trade (T) contracts again.

This is essentially a clear and simple explanation of the *business cycle,* or the *credit cycle,* as it is sometimes called. While the transition period lasts, the increase in the volume of trade (T) produces a temporary increase in PT (real GDP), followed by a bust in which both the volume of trade (T) and real GDP contract again. At the end of the process, GDP is only higher in nominal terms because of the increase in the price level (P).

Fisher was convinced that the duration of the transition period (or business cycle) would always be short-lived because there would always be a limit as to how much the quantity of money (M) could expand. He wrote:

> *There are also other forces placing a limitation on further expansion of deposit currency and introducing a tendency to contraction. Not only is the amount of deposit currency limited both by law and by prudence to a certain maximum multiple of the amount of banks reserves; but bank reserves are themselves limited by the amount of money available for use as reserves.*[5]

This is important. In 1912, the legal requirement for banks to hold liquidity reserves against their deposits and the legal requirement for the Fed to hold gold to back the paper currency it printed both limited the "further expansion of deposit currency" (i.e., money). Both those constraints have long since been removed. As discussed in Chapter 1, the banks no longer are required to hold meaningful liquidity reserves and the Fed does not back its Federal Reserve notes with gold. That means the amount of credit that can now be created is practically infinite and that the transition period during which the volume of trade (T) (and GDP) can expand is much longer than when Fisher wrote *The Purchasing Power of Money.* The implications of this change are enormous. They are explored later in this chapter and throughout the rest of this book.

There is one other aspect of the quantity theory of money that is important to understand. This theory is concerned with the impact that a change in the quantity of money (*M*) has on the price level (*P*). It does not preclude the possibility, however, that other factors in addition to the quantity of money can also affect prices. Fisher puts it as follows: "The effects of *M* are blended with the effects of changes in other factors . . . just as the effects of gravity upon a falling body are blended with the effects of the resistance of the atmosphere."[6]

It will be essential to keep this in mind when considering the implications of the quantity theory of credit because there has been one development other than the extraordinary proliferation of credit that has had a truly extraordinary impact on prices during recent decades, *globalization*. Globalization has resulted in a 95 percent decline in the marginal cost of labor in a relatively short span of time. Not long ago, blue collar workers in Michigan were paid a wage of $200 per day to work on an automobile assembly line. Today, the same job can be done in China or India at the cost of $5 per day per worker. That collapse in the price of labor represents one of the greatest upheavals in prices in history. As will be explained over the following pages, had the price of labor not collapsed, the world would have been beset by hyperinflation long ago.

The Purchasing Power of Money is an extraordinary book. Fisher writes persuasively and with remarkable clarity. The reader closes the book sharing Fisher's belief that "we find nothing to interfere with the truth of the quantity theory that variations in money (*M*) produce normally proportional changes in prices."[7]

The Rise and Fall of Monetarism

Milton Friedman was the most forceful advocate of the Quantity Theory of Money during the second half of the last century. His work on the subject during the 1960s and 1970s won a large academic following and, eventually, persuaded policymakers that they could control the rate of inflation by targeting the growth of the money supply—that is, the quantity of money.

This school of thought, which became known as *monetarism,* achieved its greatest influence on policy during the early 1980s. At that time, governments in both the United States and the United Kingdom adopted formal targets that restricted money supply growth. Those policies were successful. The rate of inflation fell sharply in both countries.

As the 1980s progressed, however, monetarism lost credibility as it become clear that monetary targeting did not always deliver the expected results. The price level did not change in exact accordance with the quantity of money as the theory held it must. In particular, the velocity of money (*V*) proved to be erratic and unpredictable. It rose from less than four times in 1960 to seven times in 1980, then oscillated between six and seven times for the next 15 years before moving up to ten times just before the global crisis began.

Monetarists blamed the divergence between theory and practice on the changing nature of money. By definition, the money supply comprised two components, money in circulation and demand deposits at banks. The monetarists understood that the nature of money had begun to change. In the 1980s, they began to look for a broader definition of money that would encompass other money-like instruments in addition to cash and demand deposits. New *monetary aggregates* were devised:

- M1 was the name given to the traditional definition of money, i.e., currency plus demand deposits.
- M2 includes M1 plus time deposits and money market funds.
- M3 includes M2 plus time deposits and term repos.
- MZM, money zero maturity, includes M2 less time deposits, but including money market funds.

And there were others.

It had been hoped that some broader definition of money would produce the stable relationship between the quantity of money and the price level that the quantity theory of money asserted should exist. None of the new monetary aggregates succeeded in generating the results anticipated, however. Consequently, the credibility of monetarism diminished and its use as a policy tool fell off.

Part of the reason that monetarism failed to produce the anticipated results was due to changes brought about by globalization. Beginning in the early 1980s, there was a marked increase in international trade and cross-border capital flows. As a result, the structure of the U.S. economy began to change. In particular, the sudden and unprecedented expansion of the U.S. trade deficit, which reflected the economy's increasing integration with the rest of the world, made it more difficult to establish a steady, causal relationship between the domestic money supply and domestic economic output.

Nevertheless, the monetarists would have met with greater success if they had broadened their definition of money even further. Their mistake was to fail to see that there *is* no distinction between fiat money and credit. They should have included all dollar-denominated credit instruments in their definition of money. Or, put differently, they should have replaced money with credit in the equation of exchange, because by the 1980s there was less and less difference between the two. Now there is essentially none.

Money, it is said, must meet three criteria. It must be (1) a medium of exchange, (2) a store of value, and (3) a unit of account. And, in order to serve as a medium of exchange, money needs to be liquid, or in other words, easily accessible and transferable. Before 1968, there was a clear difference between money and credit. Until then, dollars were backed by gold, so the dollars in circulation represented a claim on a commodity with intrinsic value. Credit, by contrast, was merely an obligation to repay a certain amount of money. After 1968, that distinction vanished. Dollars no longer represent a claim on a real commodity. Today, if a person attempts to redeem a dollar by presenting it to the Treasury Department, the government has no obligation to give that person anything other than another dollar. Dollars now, therefore, are simply credit instruments that do not pay interest.

Meanwhile, because of financial innovation, credit has become more like money. Most credit instruments have long met the three criteria that define money. They can serve as a medium of exchange, they are a store of value, and they are a unit of account. In the past, however, they were not liquid. Now they are. The *repo market* makes them liquid. The repurchase market allows the owner of any credit instrument to obtain cash immediately by agreeing to repurchase that asset at a specified date in the future. Treasury bonds, municipal bonds, corporate bonds, GSE debt, and asset-backed securities are all now completely liquid. In other words, the entire $52 trillion in credit market debt outstanding is liquid and, therefore, money-like.

So, with money having become more like credit and credit having become more like money, there is little point in making any distinction between the two. Moreover, in recent decades, the quantity of credit has become so great relative to the quantity of money that it has made money irrelevant.

The Quantity Theory of Credit

The principal reason that monetarism became incapable of achieving the results expected of it was that money became indistinguishable from credit. After 1968, the thing that had been money, gold, made up a smaller and smaller fraction of the money supply, so small that it became completely irrelevant to the overall economy. It is the credit supply, not the money supply, that counts now. Therefore, the quantity theory of money must be revised to incorporate that change. Since credit has replaced money as the key economic variable, credit must be substituted for money in the equation of exchange, as follows:

$$CV = PT$$

where:

C = Total credit market debt
V = Velocity (the average rate of turnover of credit)
P = Price level (the weighted average of all prices)
T = Trade (the volume of trade)

The lesson to be learned from $CV = PT$ is that PT, that is, GDP, is driven by credit. Credit growth pushes up nominal GDP in the same way that an increase in the quantity of money did in the past, by causing an increase in the price level. However, in our system, where fiat money allows unlimited credit creation, credit growth can also push up the volume of trade (T) and, therefore, real GDP, for a very long period of time, producing a much larger economic boom than was possible within a commodity-money based system that Fisher understood.

When Fisher wrote about the quantity theory of money, increases in the money supply were constrained by the legal requirement that dollars be backed by gold and by prudential regulations that required banks to hold liquidity reserves. Those constraints have long since been removed. Now there is effectively no limit on how much credit can be created.

In Fisher's day, an increase in the quantity of money caused a proportionate and lasting increase in the price level, but only a temporary increase in real GDP. The increase in real GDP was transitory because an increase in money only boosted the volume of trade (T) for a short time before money ceased to expand and the volume of trade (T) and real GDP contracted again.

In the modern age of fiat money, the expansion of credit can go on far longer. As long as credit continues to expand, the volume of trade (and therefore real GDP) will continue to expand. As long as credit growth continues, the transition period that Fisher believed to be short-lived never comes to an end.

The quantity theory of money held that (all other things unchanged) an increase in the money supply would cause an increase in prices and a short-lived boom and bust cycle that, in the end, would leave nominal GDP higher, but real GDP unchanged. The quantity theory of credit differs from the older theory in only one important respect. It contends that, under the current system of fiat money, the boom and bust cycle is much longer because now credit can expand for far longer than the money supply could within in the commodity money based system of the past.

The "transition period" of the boom is far longer, but it is not infinite. It ends when credit ceases to expand. Ultimately, every credit-induced economic boom ends when asset prices become too inflated and industrial production becomes too excessive relative to the income of the public. The boom can only last if wages keep pace with asset prices and industrial output. When they don't, the public becomes incapable of servicing its debt. Then the transition period ends, the boom goes into reverse and the depression begins.

Why must the boom go into reverse? Why could economic growth not just flatten out rather than contract? Consider first the impact that rising asset prices have on an economy. When credit expands, it causes asset prices to rise. For instance, when home prices are rising, homeowners can refinance and extract equity from their homes, and, therefore, spend more. Higher spending boosts the economy, creating jobs, profits, and tax revenues. When credit stops expanding, home prices stop rising and additional equity extraction becomes impossible. At that point, homeowners have to spend less than before. Reduced spending causes the economy to contract, and jobs, profits, and tax revenues are lost.

That is only one example of why the boom goes into reverse when credit stops expanding. The dynamics are similar for other sectors of the economy as well. When business credit expands, companies invest more and hire more employees. The overall economy benefits. When business credit ceases to expand, companies will not be able to increase their rate of investment or hire as many people as before. Consequently, the economy will slow.

Those dynamics are typically made worse by the fact that credit rarely ceases to expand until past loans begin to default in large numbers. Generally, credit growth goes on so long that it pushes asset prices to unaffordable levels on the one hand and it causes industrial production to exceed market demand on the other. At that point, not only does credit cease to expand, it begins to contract (at least for the affected sectors). The credit boom then becomes a credit bust as consumption and investment contract.

In the United States, total credit market debt expanded every year without exception between 1947 and 2008. That created an extraordinary period of prosperity in which credit growth drove economic growth. The New Depression began in 2008 when that credit could not be repaid and, as a result, credit began to contract.

Credit and Inflation

Between 1968, the year the United States moved to a system of fiat money, and 2007, the last year of the economic boom, the U.S. money supply (M1) increased from $190 billion to $1,372 billion, an average growth rate of 5.3 percent a year. Over the same period, total credit expanded at an average annual rate of 9.6 percent, from $1.3 trillion to $48 trillion.

If credit has usurped the place of money, as is contended here, why did this incredible expansion of credit not produce extraordinarily high rates of inflation given the revised equation of exchange, $CV = PT$?

In fact, it did. There are three kinds, or categories, of inflation: asset price inflation, commodity price inflation, and consumer price inflation excluding food and energy. Each one must be considered separately.

Asset price inflation in the United States has been acute. As described in the last chapter, stock prices rose 14 times between 1982 and 2000, while the median price of a home rose from $64,000 in 1980 to $257,000 in 2007.

There have also been two rounds of extreme commodity price inflation. The first took place during the 1970s immediately after the United States moved to a fiat money system and the second between 2002 and mid-2008 when rapid growth in credit in the United States occurred simultaneously with aggressive fiat money creation abroad.

During the 1970s, wage rates in the United States rose to keep pace with the high rates of commodity price inflation. Rising commodity prices and rising wage rates quickly translated into higher prices for industrial good, which are reported in the "core" Consumer Price Index (CPI), which excludes food and energy costs. During the second commodity spike that began in 2002, that did not occur. U.S. wage rates could not rise because of globalization. Globalization resulted in a 95 percent drop in the marginal cost of labor by bringing a billion people from the developing world into the global industrial workforce. Never in history had the price of labor fallen so far, so fast. Extreme labor price deflation prevented surging commodity prices from spilling over into higher rates of core CPI. Had globalization not occurred at that time, the rapid credit growth in the United States would have produced crippling rates of inflation in the 1980s and the 1990s and the 2000s, just as it did during the 1970s. The economy would have remained marred in the stagflation of the 1970s—or worse, been decimated by hyperinflation. Instead, the combination of extraordinary credit growth and a collapse in labor costs created a multidecade economic boom that transformed the world.

Conclusion

Chapter 3, Creditopia, described what a $50 trillion expansion of credit did to the U.S. economy. Viewed through the $CV = PT$ framework, it is clear that the vast expansion of credit drove a very long economic boom characterized by surging asset prices, surging commodity prices, and an increased volume of trade. Consumer prices inflation (excluding food and energy) remained relatively contained because the price of industrial goods was depressed by a separate, independent factor, the collapse of the marginal cost of labor brought about by globalization.

The New Depression began in 2008 when credit could expand no further. The boom then went into reverse. Asset and commodity prices plunged, spending slumped, and debt defaults destroyed such enormous quantities of capital that the financial system narrowly avoided collapse. At that point, the government intervened in order to prevent a collapse into a New Great Depression. Chapter 5 will look at the government's policy response through the framework of the quantity theory of credit.

The debt-fueled economic paradigm that has driven the U.S. economy for the last 40 years has begun to collapse. The quantity theory of credit implies that economic disaster will only be averted if credit begins to expand again. Chapter 6 looks at the U.S. economy sector by sector to determine whether it will. Based on that assessment, Chapter 7 describes how this crisis is likely to ultimately play out.

Notes

1. Ludwig von Mises, *Human Action* (New Haven, CT: Yale University,1949), p. 563.
2. Irving Fisher, *The Purchasing Power of Money: Its Determination and Relation to Credit, Interest and Crises* (New York: The Macmillan Company, 1912).
3. Fisher, pp. 16–17.
4. Fisher, p. 153.
5. Fisher, p. 64.
6. Fisher, p. 159.
7. Fisher, p. 183.

CHAPTER 5

The Policy Response: Perpetuating the Boom

I would like to say to Milton [Friedman] and Anna [Schwartz]: Regarding the Great Depression. You're right, we [the Fed] did it. We're very sorry. But thanks to you, we won't do it again.

—Fed Governor Ben Bernanke[1]

What a pity that Bernanke did not read Ludwig von Mises instead of Milton Friedman in graduate school! If he had, he would have known that credit creates the boom and that all booms bust. Instead, he was taught that the Great Depression occurred because the Fed made two mistakes:

1. It increased interest rates in late 1928 to slow down the stock market bubble.
2. It did not print money and bail out all the banks when the credit the banks had extended could not be repaid.

By putting into practice those mistaken lessons drawn from the Great Depression, Bernanke and his colleagues at the Federal Reserve have brought upon the United States and the world the New Depression. Guided by a flawed interpretation of historic events, the Fed, beginning with Greenspan and continuing under Bernanke, has done absolutely everything in its power to perpetuate the credit boom in the United States. As a result, they have created the greatest global credit bubble in history.

Those who want to understand what lies ahead must understand this: the Fed's one and only policy has been and will continue to be to perpetuate the boom by ensuring that credit continues to expand. Once that is understood, it is much easier to predict future government policy and to forecast how that policy will impact the economy and asset prices.

This chapter examines how the Fed's determination to perpetuate the boom shapes its policy response to the New Depression. Later chapters will consider what that means for the future.

The Credit Cycle

The Austrian economists provided the best explanation for the business cycle, the alternating boom and bust pattern that has characterized the economic process in capitalist economies since the beginning of the Industrial Revolution. They identified credit expansion as the catalyst.

This theory was expounded over several thousand pages by Ludwig von Mises in *The Theory of Money and Credit* (1912) and *Human Action* (Yale University, 1949). Murray Rothbard summed it up nicely in one paragraph in his *America's Great Depression* (1963) as follows:

> *Thus, bank credit expansion sets into motion the business cycle in all its phases: the inflationary boom, marked by expansion of the money supply and by malinvestment; the crisis, which arrives when credit expansion ceases and malinvestments become evident; and the depression recovery, the necessary adjustment process by which the economy returns to the most efficient ways of satisfying consumer desires.*[2]

The two most important facts to understand about the global economic crisis that began in 2008 and the government's policy response to it are: (1) the Austrian cycle theory is correct; and (2) the government's policy is to prevent the credit expansion from ever ceasing. In other words, the government's policy is to perpetuate the economic boom brought on by credit expansion by making sure that credit continues to expand, so that the day of reckoning (i.e., the crisis/depression) never occurs. That strategy has directed the actions undertaken by the government thus far during this crisis and it will continue to dictate the policies the government will implement as the crisis continues to unfold.

A third important fact to understand is that if the government fails and credit does contract significantly, then the New Depression will become a great deal harsher.

How Have They Done so Far?

Total credit market debt (TCMD), having expanded from $1 trillion in 1964 to $52 trillion in 2008 without a single quarterly contraction, began to contract in the second quarter of 2009. Over the following five quarters, credit contracted by $936 billion to $51.8 trillion. (See Exhibit 5.1.) It then began to expand again as the result of an extraordinary increase in government debt and an astonishing expansion of the central bank's balance sheet (which was needed to finance the increase in the government's debt at low interest rates). At the time of writing, TCMD had not quite expanded to its previous peak. Neither has U.S. GDP.

The federal government expanded its debt by $4.4 trillion (by 83 percent) between mid-2008 and the first quarter of 2011. The New Depression would most certainly have been a New Great Depression had it not done so. Government deficit spending provided the aggregate demand that kept the economy from breaking down when much of the private sector became incapable of repaying its debt. By borrowing and spending the government provided very direct support—life support—to the economy. The contribution made by the Federal Reserve was just as important but far more complex.

EXHIBIT 5.1 Total Credit Market Debt Not Yet Back to Its Peak

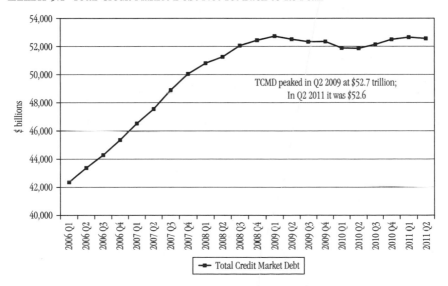

Source: Federal Reserve, *Flow of Funds Accounts of the United States, second quarter 2011*

Monetary Omnipotence and the Limits Thereof

Ben Bernanke is an ardent enthusiast of the teachings of Milton Friedman, and in particular of the conclusions drawn from Friedman's famous book *A Monetary History of the United States, 1867–1960* (written with Anna Jacobson Schwartz in 1963). In one speech, Bernanke went so far as to say:

> *Milton has never been a big fan of government licensing of professions, but maybe he would make an exception in the case of monetary policymakers. With an appropriately designed licensing examination, focused heavily on the fine details of the Monetary History, perhaps we could ensure that policymakers had at least some of the appreciation of the lessons of history that always informed Milton Friedman's views on monetary policy.[3]*

Unfortunately, extraordinary as that book is, it reached the wrong conclusions regarding the causes of the Great Depression. Friedman failed to recognize that a credit bubble set off by the breakdown of the Gold Standard at the beginning of World War I had caused the Roaring Twenties to roar. All the fiat money and government debt created during the war set off the boom; and the boom ended when the credit could not be repaid in 1930. Once the boom was underway, there was nothing the Fed could have done to prevent the bust—although it could have delayed the bust and exacerbated the boom by printing money and bailing out the banks in 1930 and 1931. In that case, a bigger bust would have occurred later.

Friedman's mistaken conclusions infected the Fed and fueled that institution's delusions of omnipotence. The idea that everything would be fine so long as credit continued to expand shaped Fed policy from the time that Greenspan took over from Paul Volcker as Fed chairman in 1987. And, for quite a long time, the implementation of that philosophy produced the desired results. Every time the economy slowed or a crisis erupted, the Fed cut interest rates or took other steps that encouraged credit expansion and the economy reaccelerated. The reality, however, was that each intervention by the Fed simply created greater distortions throughout the economy as more and more credit was misallocated into unviable investments or simply wasted on consumption. The economy grew, but it grew in an unhealthy and unsustainable manner. Asset price bubbles formed and reshaped the structure of the economy. The NASDAQ bubble misallocated credit into the telecommunications and Internet sectors. When it popped, the Fed orchestrated the property bubble, which misallocated even more credit into housing. When

EXHIBIT 5.2 The Federal Funds Rate

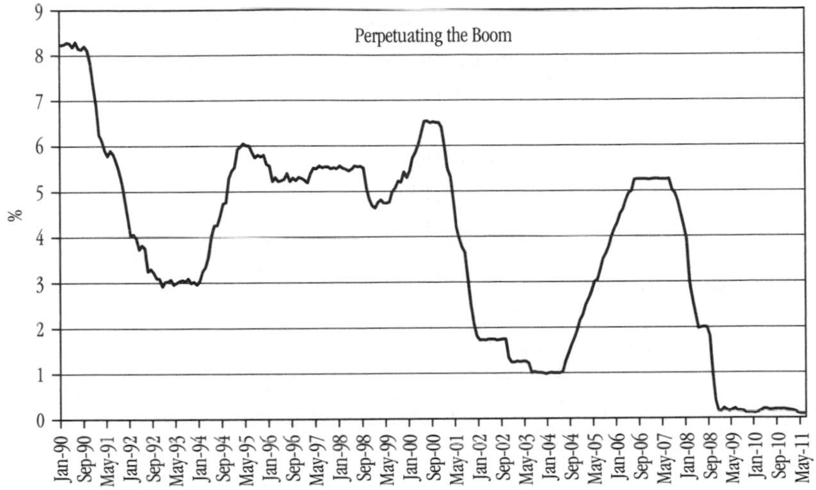

Source: Economagic

the subprime loans could not be repaid, the losses produced a systemic banking crisis and forced the effective nationalization of Fannie Mae and Freddie Mac.

Next, Bernanke cut interest rates to zero (see Exhibit 5.2), but that was not enough. It was no longer just a matter of ensuring that credit continued to expand. The credit market was imploding under the losses on defaulting and non-performing assets. Credit began to contract and the economy plunged into crisis. At that point the Fed had only one tool left, the printing press. Thus began quantitative easing (QE).

The Balance Sheet of the Federal Reserve

The Fed has a balance sheet. It is published weekly on its website under the heading "Factors Affecting Reserve Balances" at the following website, www .federalreserve.gov/releases/h41/. An easier to read format is provided quarterly as Table L.108 in the Fed's Flow of Funds release, www.federalreserve .gov/releases/z1/default.htm.

A tremendous amount can be learned from examining how the central bank's balance sheet changes over time. At the end of 2006, before the problems in the financial market began, the Fed held $908 billion of assets, of which 86 percent were Treasury securities (i.e., government debt). Its liabilities totaled $893 billion. Of that amount, 86 percent was currency outside banks, or, in other words, the paper notes the Fed had printed in the past.

By the fourth quarter of 2007, jitters over growing problems with subprime loans caused liquidity conditions in the financial markets to tighten as lenders became more cautious about extending credit to other financial institutions. At that time, the Fed began making loans to domestic banks through its discount window, a conventional practice for a central bank. By the fourth quarter of 2008, however, the amount lent had reached $544 billion, well beyond a conventional level.

The Fed also began injecting liquidity into the markets through unconventional means. In the first quarter of 2008, the Fed started extending credit to brokers and dealers through a new program called the primary dealer credit facility (PDCF). That lending program peaked at $200 billion in the third quarter of 2008. From the following quarter, the Fed began providing funding through a number of facilities to help rescue Bear Stearns and AIG, mostly through vehicles named Maiden Lane I, II, and III. These peaked at $118 billion in the first quarter of 2009.

Next, during the third quarter of 2008, came a $100 billion credit line through the Asset-Backed Commercial Paper Money Mutual Market Fund Liquidity Facility (AMLF). Finally, in the fourth quarter of 2008, the Fed extended $333 billion in credit through the Commercial Paper Funding Facility (CPFF), while providing $554 billion in U.S. dollar liquidity to other central banks through currency swaps.

This barrage of emergency lending by the Fed was necessary to prevent the financial system from melting down altogether. So many financial institutions were in crisis—Bear Stearns, AIG, Lehman Brothers, Fannie Mae, and Freddie Mac—or rumored to be (almost all the rest of the industry) that any institution that did have liquidity available to lend was afraid to do so. Had the Fed not stepped in and made funds available, the system would not have survived. In a report published in 2011, the Government Accountability Office wrote:

> On numerous occasions in 2008 and 2009, the Federal Reserve Board invoked emergency authority under the Federal Reserve Act of 1913 to authorize new broad-based programs and financial assistance to individual institutions to stabilize financial markets. Loans outstanding for the emergency programs peaked at more than $1 trillion in late 2008.[4]

These programs or, at least, most of them preceded the beginning of QE. At that time, the Fed had not yet begun to aggressively create money to obtain the funding it provided to the financial markets. Instead, it sold some of the government bonds in its portfolio to raise the cash it needed; and, in the third quarter of 2008, it obtained a $300 billion loan from the Treasury Department.

Quantitative easing began near the end of 2008. From that point, the Fed began buying credit instruments from the banks and paying for them by depositing money (money freshly created for the purpose) into the accounts in which banks held their liquidity reserves at the Fed. As discussed in Chapter 1, those reserves had steadily dwindled to next to nothing by the time the crisis began. That suddenly changed. They jumped from $33 billion in mid-2008 to $860 billion by the end of that year. By September 2011 they had grown to $1.6 trillion.

Quantitative Easing: Round One

Quantitative easing is a euphemism for fiat money creation. The "quantity" referred to is the amount of fiat money in existence. The creation of additional fiat money "eases" the liquidity conditions and lowers the cost of borrowing in the credit markets by adding to the supply of money available to borrow. Once the Fed has lowered the federal funds rate to 0 percent, QE is its only remaining policy option for stimulating the economy.

During the first round of quantitative easing (QE1), the Fed focused on buying agency- and GSE-backed securities from the banks. Those assets were primarily the debt that had been issued or guaranteed by Fannie and Freddie. The program was announced on November 25, 2008, during a quarter in which (as we know now) the U.S. economy was contracting at an annual rate of 8.9 percent. The Federal Reserve press release read:

> *The Federal Reserve announced on Tuesday that it will initiate a program to purchase the direct obligations of housing-related government-sponsored enterprises (GSEs)—Fannie Mae, Freddie Mac, and the Federal Home Loan Banks—and mortgage-backed securities (MBS) backed by Fannie Mae, Freddie Mac, and Ginnie Mae. Spreads of rates on GSE debt and on GSE-guaranteed mortgages have widened appreciably of late. This action is being taken to reduce the cost and increase the availability of credit for the purchase of houses, which in turn should support housing markets and foster improved conditions in financial markets more generally.*
>
> *Purchases of up to $100 billion in GSE direct obligations under the program will be conducted with the Federal Reserve's primary dealers through a series of competitive auctions and will begin next week. Purchases of up to $500 billion in MBS will be conducted*

*by asset managers selected via a competitive process with a goal
of beginning these purchases before year-end. Purchases of both
direct obligations and MBS are expected to take place over several
quarters.*[5]

The program that was announced on November 25, 2008, was fundamentally different than those that had come before. The funds that the Fed
would use to acquire this $600 billion of GSE and GSE-backed debt was
to be created from thin air instead of being raised by selling government
bonds already on the Fed's balance sheet. This program was to be funded
entirely by fiat money creation.

This resort to money creation should not have come as a surprise
to anyone. In a speech six years earlier, Bernanke had proclaimed that
printing money was a tool that the Fed could and would use to prevent
deflation if that became necessary after the central bank had exhausted
its more traditional policy of lowering the federal funds rate, once that
rate had been reduced to 0 percent. In that speech, he referred to "Milton
Friedman's famous 'helicopter drop' of money" metaphor, which Friedman
had used to explain how money creation causes prices to rise. This earned
Bernanke the nickname *Helicopter Ben*.[6]

And, so, at the end of 2008, the Fed's helicopters took to the air
and began showering the economy with newly created money. Then, on
March 18, 2009, the Fed expanded this program by more than 200 percent
to $1.75 trillion. The announcement read:

*To provide greater support to mortgage lending and housing markets,
the Committee decided today to increase the size of the Federal Reserve's
balance sheet further by purchasing up to an additional $750 bil-
lion of agency mortgage-backed securities, bringing its total purchases
of these securities to up to $1.25 trillion this year, and to increase its
purchases of agency debt this year by up to $100 billion to a total of
up to $200 billion. Moreover, to help improve conditions in private
credit markets, the Committee decided to purchase up to $300 billion
of longer-term Treasury securities over the next six months.*[7]

Before the first round of QE began, the Fed held roughly $900 billion
of assets. When it ended on March 31, 2010, the Fed's balance sheet had
more than doubled to $2.3 trillion. There was no precedent for fiat money
creation on this scale in the United States during peacetime.

By then, 53 percent of the Fed's assets ($1.2 trillion) were agency- and
GSE-backed securities. Treasury Securities accounted for a further 33 percent.

The other emergency programs had begun to wind down by then. On the liabilities side of the Fed's balance sheet, the reserve deposits of financial institutions accounted for 46 percent of the total, with currency outside banks making up a further 38 percent (or $883 billion).

What Did QE1 Accomplish?

First, it allowed the financial sector to begin to reduce its excessive leverage. During QE1, the Fed bought $1.75 trillion worth of debt, primarily from the financial sector. Largely as a result of Fed purchases, the debt of the financial sector declined by $2.5 trillion or by 15 percent between November 2008 and March 2010. Swapping GSE and GSE-backed debt for cash greatly improved the financial position of the sector.

Second, by acquiring this amount of debt, the Fed pushed up the price of those debt instruments and thereby drove down their yields relative to where they would have been had the Fed not intervened. This produced two important benefits. First, the higher prices on those debt instruments improved the balance sheets of all the other owners of that debt (primarily banks), thereby improving their solvency. Second, Fed purchases supported the property market by holding down the yields on the debt issued by Fannie and Freddie, which determine the cost consumers pay for mortgages.

Finally, QE1 helped drive U.S. stock prices higher by improving market liquidity and by improving market sentiment. The initial announcement of $600 billion in QE at the end of November 2008 gave the Dow Jones Industrial Average only a short-lived boost before the market resumed plunging. (See Exhibit 5.3.) However, when the Fed announced that the program would be expanded by an addition $1.15 trillion, the Dow began to surge, rising more than 50 percent between the announcement date, March 18, 2009, and the completion of QE1 on March 31, 2010.

The recovery of stock prices cannot be attributed solely to QE. Other factors also contributed to the rebound. TARP had been enacted in October 2008 and was infusing hundreds of billions into the financial system in early 2009. The government's $787 billion stimulus program became law in February 2009. In early May, the results of the bank stress test came as a relief to markets. Nonetheless, the impact on stock prices of the creation and injection of $1.75 trillion in new fiat money into the credit market should not be underappreciated–particularly considering movements in stock prices after QE1 came to an end.

EXHIBIT 5.3 Dow Jones Industrial Average

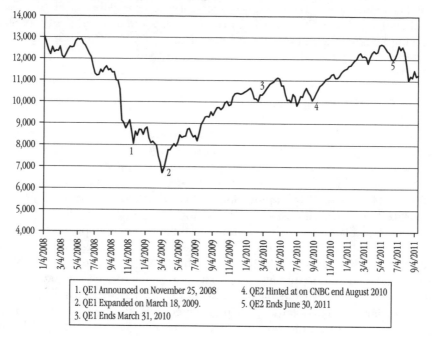

1. QE1 Announced on November 25, 2008	4. QE2 Hinted at on CNBC end August 2010
2. QE1 Expanded on March 18, 2009.	5. QE2 Ends June 30, 2011
3. QE1 Ends March 31, 2010	

Source: St. Louis Fed

Quantitative Easing: Round Two

Five weeks after QE1 ended on March 31, 2010, the U.S. stock market experienced a *flash crash* when, in one day, stock prices plummeted 10 percent before recovering to close down only 3 percent on the day. By early July the stock market was down 14 percent from its post-QE1 peak of 11,205 on April 26. That drop destroyed trillions of dollars in paper wealth, producing a negative wealth effect that immediately impacted consumption. The 2010 "soft patch" had begun. By August, most economic indicators were flashing red, and concerns over the risks of a double-dip recession began to take hold.

In late July, Fed governors began dropping hints that a new round of quantitative easing (QE2) was on the way. When Fed Chairman Bernanke confirmed as much in late August, the stock market took off again, rising to a post-crisis peak above 12,600 soon after QE2 ended on June 30, 2011. Higher stock prices created a positive wealth effect that boosted consumption, and the economy reaccelerated from the summer soft patch.

The second round of QE was officially announced following the Fed's FOMC meeting in early November. The Fed would buy $600 billion of U.S. government bonds with newly created money. By the time

QE2 ended in mid-2011, the Fed's assets had grown to $2.9 trillion. That amount was composed of $1.6 trillion in Treasury securities and $1.0 trillion in agency- and GSE-backed securities. That meant the U.S. central bank owned 16 percent of all U.S. government bonds held by the public and 13 percent of all the agency- and GSE-backed securities outstanding. Of the Fed's liabilities, 56 percent were depository institutions reserves ($1.6 trillion) and 34 percent was currency outside banks ($934 billion), the latter having increased by $200 billion, or 26 percent, since the end of 2007.

Monetizing the Debt

QE2 did drive up stock prices. Its purpose was to drive up stock prices. That was not its only purpose, however, or even its primary purpose. The second round of QE was required to finance the U.S. government's gaping budget deficit.

In 2009, federal government expenditure came to 25 percent of GDP, the highest since World War II. Federal government tax revenues amounted to only 14.9 percent of GDP, however. That was the lowest tax intake relative to GDP since 1950. Expenditures surged during the crisis due to spending on stimulus programs and the automatic stabilizers such as unemployment insurance that kick in during an economic downturn. Tax revenues fell sharply due to lower capital gains taxes and tax cuts that were part of the stimulus programs. The outcome was a budget deficit equivalent to just over 10 percent of GDP, which amounted to $1.4 trillion.

That budget deficit kept the United States economy from spiraling into a severe depression that year. Had the government been forced to balance its budget (due to a balanced budget amendment, for instance) the U.S. economy would have been $1.4 trillion smaller that year than it was. Instead of contracting by 3.5 percent compared with 2008 as it actually did, the economy would have contracted by 13.5 percent in 2009. In fact, it would have contracted even more than that, since the reduction in government spending would have had a significant multiplier effect. Very conservatively, the economy would have shrunk by 15 percent. In that scenario, unemployment would most probably have hit 20 percent. Then, in all likelihood, things would have become much worse the following year.

Every economy is composed of four major components: personal consumption expenditure, business investment, net trade, and government spending. In the United States, those four generally break down as follows:

1. Personal consumption expenditure, 70 percent of GDP
2. Business investment, 16 percent
3. Net trade, −5 percent
4. Government spending, 19 percent

Net trade deducts from GDP because imports into the United States exceed exports from the United States. This has been the case every year since 1975.

In an earlier era when gold was money, there was a limited amount of money in the economy. Then, if the government borrowed money to finance a budget deficit, it left less money for individuals and businesses to borrow. As a result, it pushed up interest rates. In that case, the government borrowing was said to "crowd out" the private sector from the credit markets, resulting in less investment and less economic growth. Conversely, a reduction in government deficit spending and borrowing caused interest rates to fall, to the benefit of the broader economy.

That was when gold was money. Things have changed. Then, governments could not create money. Now they do. Now, it is no longer only the demand for money that determines interest rates. It is also the supply of money being created by the central bank. During the year ended September 30, 2011, the U.S. budget deficit was 8.6 percent of GDP, or $1.3 trillion. Despite the massive government borrowing that was required to fund that deficit, the interest rate the government pays on its benchmark bond is 2 percent, which is extraordinarily low. The government demand to borrow money is very high, but the government supply of new fiat money (i.e., the money created by the Fed) is also extraordinarily high. Fiat money creation is financing the government's budget deficit. When a central bank creates money and uses it to finance the government's budget deficit, it is said that the central bank is *monetizing the debt*. With QE1 and QE2, the Fed monetized part the U.S. government debt. That is the main reason U.S. government bond yields—and all other interest rates in the country which are benchmarked off the government bond yield—are so low.

That means, in this age of paper money, that if the U.S. government reduces its deficit and borrows less, interest rates will not fall as they would have in the past. Interest rates are already at rock-bottom levels as a result of the Fed creating money and monetizing the debt. That is the monetary side of this issue. The fiscal repercussions of a reduction in government spending have not changed, however. If the government spends less (or taxes more), the economy will contract by the amount of the reduction in spending plus a multiplier. There will be no offsetting benefit from lower interest rates, as there would have been in the past. Therefore, a reduction in government spending will not boost business investment or personal consumption. In fact, it will reduce both because less government spending will result in fewer jobs, less aggregate demand, less profits, and fewer business opportunities.

At a time when a large section of American society is demanding that the government spend less, it is crucial for everyone to understand that less government spending means that the U.S. economy will become smaller and that unemployment will rise. The economy no longer functions as it did when gold was money.

The Role of the Trade Deficit

For 12 years the U.S. current account deficit financed the U.S. budget deficit, and financed it at low interest rates. (The current account is composed primarily of the balance of trade, but also includes the balance of income and current transfers.) As described in Chapter 2, every country's balance of payments must balance. Therefore, a country with a large current account deficit will also have a large, offsetting inflow of capital on its financial account. From 1996 to 2008, the capital inflow on the U.S. financial account (inflows that were necessary to finance the U.S. current account deficit) was much larger than the U.S. government's budget deficit. Only part of those capital inflows actually was invested directly in government debt. The rest was invested in other financial assets, causing their prices to rise and their yields to fall. Domestic investors, therefore, were incentivized to buy more government bonds than they otherwise would have for two reasons. First, there were fewer other kinds of assets left in the market to buy. Second, on a risk-adjusted basis, the yield on government bonds became more attractive relative to the depressed yields on other assets. Put differently, money is fungible. The inflow of hundreds of billions of dollar each year pushed money into all corners of the credit market, including the corner occupied by U.S. government bonds.

When the crisis erupted, the financial inflows into the United States declined because the U.S. trade deficit declined. When households defaulted on their debt, they were forced to spend less. Lower consumer spending meant a reduction in U.S. imports and, therefore, in the U.S. trade deficit and current account deficit. Meanwhile, the U.S. budget deficit more than tripled. From 2009, the money entering the United States to fund the current account deficit was no longer large enough to finance the government's budget deficit. The current account deficit fell to $380 billion, while the budget deficit blew out to $1.4 trillion. Suddenly there was a $1 trillion gap between the two. The situation did not improve meaningfully the following year. In 2010, the U.S. current account deficit, at $480 billion, pulled in $800 billion less than the amount needed to fund the government's $1.3 trillion budget deficit. (See Exhibit 5.4.)

Quantitative easing was required to plug that gap. Out of the $1.75 trillion in fiat money the Fed created during QE1, it spent $300 billion acquiring government bonds. It exchanged the remaining $1.45 trillion for GSE-related debt. The sellers of that debt received $1.45 trillion from the Fed, which they needed to invest in some other part of the credit market. During that period of market turmoil, Treasury bonds would have

EXHIBIT 5.4 The U.S. Budget Deficit and the U.S. Current Account Deficit

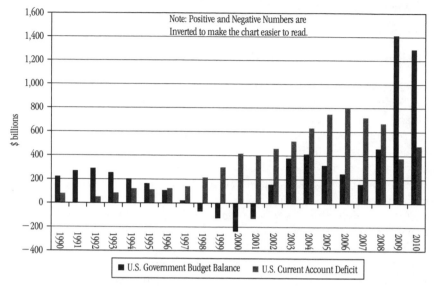

Source: Congressional Budget Office and Bureau of Economic Analysis

attracted a significant portion of that money due to the safety they offered relative to other investment opportunities at that time.

Thus, QE1 indirectly financed the budget deficit during 2009 and early 2010. With QE2, the Fed directly financed the budget deficit. The Fed spent all $600 billion it allocated for the second round of QE acquiring government bonds. In other words, during the life of QE2 from November 2010 to mid-2011 the Fed financed roughly 80 percent of the government's budget deficit with its electronic printing press.

Diminishing Returns

The Fed grew its balance sheet from roughly $900 billion soon before the launch of QE1 in November 2008 to $2.9 trillion at the completion of QE2 in mid-2011. What did this creation of $2 trillion in new fiat money accomplish?

The immediate, short-term impact on the U.S. economy was unquestionably positive. It made three important contributions. First, by acquiring assets from the financial sector, it improved that industry's solvency by pushing up asset prices and by facilitating a reduction in leverage. Second, QE pushed up stock prices, which created a wealth effect that boosted the economy. Third, it made it possible for the government to finance its extraordinarily large budget deficits at low interest rates. This was absolutely crucial because deficit spending by the government prevented the economy from collapsing into depression when large parts of the private sector became uncreditworthy and were forced to spend much less. In that respect, monetary policy was an indispensable component of fiscal policy.

There were undesirable side effects, however, even when considering only the short-term consequences of QE. Of these, the most damaging was that QE caused a spike in food prices that caused severe distress for the two billion people in the world who live on less than $2 per day. The resulting food riots kindled full-blown revolutions across North Africa and the Middle East that toppled governments and threatened to sweep away practically overnight the political and diplomatic alignments the United States had built up in that region over decades.

The increase in food prices had a mixed impact on the U.S. economy. It harmed consumers who had to pay more for food, but it benefited the country's giant agro corporations and the farmers who grew and sold the food.

In addition to pushing up food prices, QE also drove up the price of oil; and the impact on the economy of higher oil prices was almost entirely negative. Higher gasoline prices acted as a tax on the consumer and, moreover, that tax was paid to foreign oil produces, thereby exacerbating the United States trade deficit.

By the first quarter of 2011 (when QE2 was still in full swing), the cost of QE had begun to catch up to, if not overtake, its benefits. U.S. GDP grew by only 0.4 percent that quarter (on an annualized basis), in large part due to a slowdown in consumption (due to higher food and energy prices) and a pick-up in inflation. During the first half of 2011, U.S. GDP expanded by only 0.8 percent on an annualized basis.

The benefits derived from QE appear to be subject to the law of diminishing returns. That outcome should not have come as a surprise to the Fed chairman, however. In October 2003, Bernanke, in yet another speech praising Milton Friedman, made the following statement:

In particular, as Friedman told us, a monetary expansion has its more immediate effects on real variables such as output, consumption, and investment, with the bulk of these effects occurring over two to three quarters. These real effects tend to dissipate over time, however, so that at a horizon of twelve to eighteen months the effects of a monetary expansion or contraction are felt primarily on the rate of inflation.[8]

The Fed's experiment with QE very clearly supports that conclusion.

In his earlier "helicopter money" speech, Bernanke famously said that the Fed would not be out of bullets even once it had lowered the Fed

Funds rate to zero because the Fed could create money and buy assets. Given the outcome generated by $2 trillion in fiat money creation during two rounds of QE, it would be of great interest to know just how many bullets Bernanke believes the Fed has left now.

The Other Money Makers

It is important to remember that the Fed has not been alone in creating fiat money on a large scale in response to this crisis. The European Central Bank has increased its balance sheet (i.e., created euros) by 950 billion euros, or 80 percent since the crisis began (mid-2007). And the Bank of England has followed suit by growing its balance sheet by 164 billion pounds (206 percent). Even the International Monetary Fund has become a big-time fiat money creator. It expanded the amount of Special Drawing Rights (SDRs) (IMF money) in existence by a factor of ten, or roughly the equivalent of $280 billion, in the third quarter of 2009. The new SDRs were handed out to IMF member countries in proportion to their quotas (ownership stake) in the Fund and they served as a badly needed injection of global liquidity at a time when money was otherwise tight all around.

The Fed, the ECB, and the BOE printed their own currencies and used the money to buy assets denominated in their own currencies. Their purpose was to boost the domestic liquidity of each of their respective countries in order to prevent debt deflation at home.

Meanwhile, China's central bank created the equivalent of $1.7 trillion between the end of 2007 and mid-2011, using the money to more than double its foreign exchange (FX) reserves to the equivalent of $3.2 trillion. The People's Bank of China (PBOC) did this to prevent the deluge of foreign currency then entering China as a result of its current account surplus and its financial account surplus from driving up the value of the Chinese yuan. In other words, by printing yuan and using it to buy the foreign currencies that entered China, the PBOC managed to hold down the value of the yuan in order to benefit Chinese exporters. Once it had accumulated the foreign currencies, however, in order to earn income on that money, the PBOC had to buy assets denominated in the foreign currencies it had accumulated. By doing so, China's central bank pumped a significant amount of liquidity into the rest of the world. Therefore, the fiat money creation undertaken by the Fed, ECB, and BOE was targeted at boosting their domestic liquidity, whereas the fiat money creation by the PBOC had the effect of adding to the liquidity of other countries. But which other countries? Because China does not publish a breakdown of its FX reserves, only the PBOC knows for sure. (See Exhibit 5.5.)

EXIIIBIT 5.5 Annual Change in China's Foreign Exchange Reserves

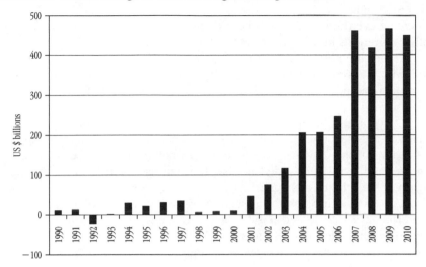

Source: IMF, International Financial Statistics

EXHIBIT 5.6 The Increase in China's Foreign Exchange Reserves as a Percentage of the Increase in Total Foreign Exchange Reserves

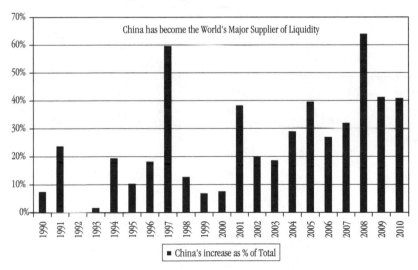

Source: IMF, International Financial Statistics

Exhibit 5.5 shows the annual increase in China's FX reserves. Throughout most of the period depicted in that chart, China's reserves grew due to the country's growing trade surplus. In 2009 and 2010, however, not only did China have a large surplus on its current account but it also had a large surplus on its financial account, equivalent to $177 billion and $221 billion in those two years, respectively. That meant the PBOC had to create even more money to hold down the value of the yuan by buying other currencies in the FX market.

During four years, 2007 to 2010, China added the equivalent of $1.8 trillion to its FX reserves, making China by far the largest contributor to international liquidity through FX reserves accumulation, as shown in Exhibit 5.6.

Of course, China was not the only country intervening in the FX markets to hold down the value of its currency. Exhibit 5.7 updates Exhibit 2.4 from Chapter 2, which listed the top 15 holders of FX reserves in 2007. Switzerland has been added to that list because of the surge in its FX reserves after the crisis began.

The Swiss franc has the reputation of being a "sound" currency, and therefore it is considered a safe haven in times of crisis. After the crisis began, so many foreign investors bought the Swiss currency that it appreciated sharply. Eventually, the Swiss central bank, the Swiss National Bank,

EXHIBIT 5.7 Foreign Exchange Reserves
Top 15 Countries in 2007 plus Switzerland

U.S.$ billions	2007	2008	2009	2010	Increase from 2007 to 2010
China	1,530	1,949	2,416	2,866	1,336
Japan	953	1,009	1,022	1,061	109
Russia	467	412	417	444	−23
Saudi Arabia	305	442	410	445	139
Taiwan	270	292	348	382	112
India	267	247	265	275	8
Korea	262	201	270	291	29
Brazil	179	193	237	287	108
Singapore	163	174	188	226	63
Hong Kong	153	182	256	269	116
Algeria	110	143	149	163	52
Malaysia	101	91	95	105	4
Mexico	87	95	100	120	33
Thailand	85	109	135	168	82
Libya	79	92	99	100	20
Switzerland	44	45	98	223	179
Subtotal					2,367
World					2,889

Source: IMF, International Financial Statistics

began to intervene on an aggressive scale. That resulted in a fivefold increase in Switzerland's FX reserves between 2007 and 2010.

Altogether, the 16 countries on this list added the equivalent of $2.4 trillion to their FX reserves during the course of 2008, 2009, and 2010, with China accounting for 56 percent of that increase.

An interesting question is, into which countries were all those reserves invested? Recall from Chapter 2 that a country cannot invest its FX reserves domestically without first converting them into the local currency, which would push up the value of that currency and defeat the whole purpose of buying the FX in the first place. Therefore, foreign FX are always invested abroad.

Exhibit 5.8 shows that while the United States had traditionally absorbed most of the increase in the world's FX reserves due to the need to finance its large current account deficit (the financial inflows financed the current account deficit), that was not the case in 2007, 2009, or 2010.

Here is a double mystery. In 2009 and 2010, the U.S. financial account surplus of $268 billion and $237 billion, respectively, was not large enough to finance the country's current account deficits of $378 billion and $470 billion, respectively, during those years. "Net Errors and Omissions" of $163 billion and $235 billion, respectively, have been inserted into the statement of the U.S. Balance of Payments in order to make it balance. In other words, it is unclear how the United States

EXHIBIT 5.8 The Annual Increase in Total Foreign Exchange Reserves vs. the U.S. Financial Account Balance, 1970 to 2007

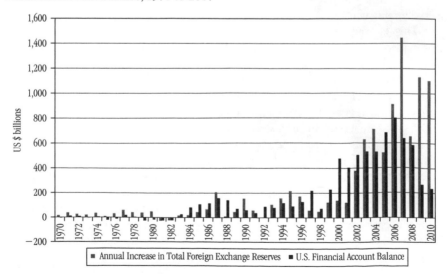

Source: IMF, International Financial Statistics

financed its current account deficits during those years. And, beyond that, even if the surplus on the financial account had been high enough to cover the current account deficit in 2009 and 2010 (i.e., $378 billion and $470 billion, respectively), the United States would have absorbed only half of the increase in the world's FX reserves in those two years. There was a similar situation in 2007.

So where did the other half of the FX reserves that were accumulated in those years go? It is a mystery. There are only so many possible explanations, however. It is possible, but unlikely, that the FX reserves weren't invested at all, but are being held in cash earning no return. It is possible— and, in fact, it is the case—that some of the reserves were used by the central banks to acquire gold; but that only accounts for a relatively small portion of the sums under consideration. They could have been invested in yen, and perhaps some of them were. That would help explain the strength of the Japanese currency during these years. Similarly, some of the reserves would have been invested in euro-denominated assets, although hopefully not in Greek, Irish, Portuguese, Spanish, or Italian government bonds. Finally, many of those reserves could have been used to supply dollar funding to dollar-starved financial institutions outside the United States during those periods of peak anxiety when dollar liquidity dried up in the financial markets outside the United States.

The gap between the increase in FX reserves and the U.S. financial account surplus for 2007 to 2010 was much larger than it had ever been before, $2.6 trillion. That is a lot of money. It had to go somewhere outside the United States. Wherever it went, it drove up asset prices, which, in turn, positively impacted the economies of the recipient countries (at least initially as it was coming in).

This chapter is about the policy response to the global crisis. On the one hand, it might be that part of this unaccounted for money was deployed intentionally to corners of the world in need of emergency liquidity. On the other hand, it might not have been. Maybe it was all just randomly invested and not part of any rescue policy. This question will remain unanswered unless China reveals where (or, at least, in which currencies) its $3.2 trillion worth of FX reserves are invested.

In any case, what is certain is that total FX reserves increased by $3.8 trillion (i.e., by 56 percent) between the end of 2007 and mid-2011. That means that central banks created roughly $3.8 trillion to accumulate those reserves. Fiat money creation on that scale and in such a short space of time most certainly had a significant impact on the global economy. As with the creation of all fiat money, its impact most probably will prove to have been very beneficial in the short term and very damaging over the long run. (See Exhibit 5.9.)

EXHIBIT 5.9 World: Total Foreign Exchange Reserves minus Gold, 1948 to mid-2011

Source: IMF, International Financial Statistics

Notes

1. At the Conference to Honor Milton Friedman, University of Chicago, November 8, 2001, on Milton Friedman's Ninetieth Birthday.
2. Murray N. Rothbard, *America's Great Depression*, Ludwig von Mises Institute, first published 1963, p. 13.
3. Remarks by Governor Ben Bernanke, At the Federal Reserve Bank of Dallas Conference on the Legacy of Milton and Rose Friedman's Free to Choose, Dallas, Texas, October 24, 2003. See also Ben Bernanke's book, *Essays on the Great Depression* (Princeton, NJ: Princeton University Press, 2000).
4. U.S. General Accounting Office. *Federal Reserve System: Opportunities Exist to Strengthen Policies and Processes for Managing Emergency Assistance*, GAO-11-696.
5. Federal Reserve Press Release, November 25, 2008, http://www.federal reserve.gov/newsevents/press/monetary/20081125b.htm.
6. Remarks by Federal Reserve Governor Ben S. Bernanke, Before the National Economists Club, Washington, DC, November 21, 2002, www.federalreserve.gov/boarddocs/speeches/2002/20021121/default.htm.
7. Federal Reserve Press Release, March 18, 2009, http://www.federalreserve.gov/newsevents/press/monetary/20090318a.htm.
8. Remarks by Governor Ben Bernanke, at the Federal Reserve Bank of Dallas Conference on the Legacy of Milton and Rose Friedman's Free to Choose, Dallas, Texas, October 24, 2003.

CHAPTER 6

Where Are We Now?

The lesson of history is emphatically that irredeemable paper money results in monetary manipulation, business distrust, a speculative condition of trade, and all the evils which flow from these conditions.

—Irving Fisher[1]

Where are we now? We are at the top of a forty-year, credit-induced economic boom without any obvious means of expanding credit further. Every boom busts. And the bust occurs when credit ceases to expand. This chapter considers why the debt of the private sector in the United States cannot expand further. Next, this chapter looks at the over-concentrated and underregulated U.S. banking sector in order to clarify exactly what is meant by "too big to fail." The chapter concludes with a discussion of the global imbalances that continue to destabilize the world. Global supply greatly exceeds sustainable demand. The gap between the two has been filled with U.S. demand, financed by debt. If credit in the United States now ceases to expand, there is a real danger that this 40-year boom will break down into a New Great Depression. Chapter 7 considers how this crisis is likely to play out over the next three years. Chapter 8 outlines the disaster scenarios.

How Bad so Far?

Fourteen million Americans are unemployed and a further 9 million cannot find the full-time employment they seek. The unemployment rate is 9.1 percent and the underemployment rate is 16.5 percent. Even more damaging to society than the number of people out of work is the duration of their joblessness, which, at 40 weeks, is twice as long as that during any other economic downturn since the late 1940s when records began.

Millions of Americans have lost their homes through foreclosures. Home prices have fallen by more than 30 percent on average across the nation. And owners' equity in homes has fallen to a record low of 39 percent. The failure of Fannie Mae and Freddie Mac and their placement into *conservatorship* by the government has resulted in the effective nationalization of more than half of the entire U.S. mortgage market. The government bailed out the banking sector and the automobile industry and took over AIG, the insurance giant.

Federal tax revenues fell by 10 percent between fiscal year 2007 and fiscal year 2011, while outlays surged by 32 percent. That has resulted in a cumulative budget deficit of $4 trillion in just three years. The size of the Fed's balance sheet has tripled due to fiat money creation.

This book is called *The New Depression* not only because of the severity of the economic downturn thus far but also because of the calamity that still lies ahead if a permanent solution is not put in place in time to prevent it. The risk of such an outcome is much greater than is generally understood.

Credit Growth Drove Economic Growth

One of the themes of this book is that credit growth has become the driver of economic growth during recent decades. Exhibit 6.1 strongly supports that view. It shows credit growth and economic growth, both adjusted for inflation, from 1952 to 2010.

EXHIBIT 6.1 Credit Growth Drives Economic Growth

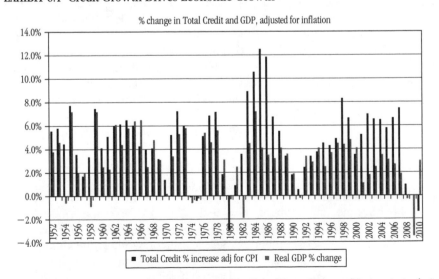

% change in Total Credit and GDP, adjusted for inflation

Total Credit % increase adj for CPI   Real GDP % change

Source: Federal Reserve, *Flow of Funds Accounts of the United States*, Bureau of Economic Analysis

First notice that over those 59 years, credit growth exceeded GDP growth in all but 16 years. Next, note that there were only 12 years during which credit expanded by less than 2 percent, and in every instance except one, 1970, such weak credit growth was accompanied by a recession, either in the same year or in the following year. In 1970, GDP grew, but only by 0.2 percent. (Credit contracted in 2010 while the GDP expanded. It is too early to judge whether 2011 will be a recession year. During the first half of 2011, GDP expanded by only 0.8 percent, despite the stimulus provided by the second round of quantitative easing, which injected approximately $500 billion into the economy during the first half of the year.)

It is also significant that the gap between credit growth and economic growth expanded after dollars ceased to be backed by gold in 1968. From 1952 to 1968, credit grew by 5 percent a year on average, while the GDP grew by 3.9 percent, a gap of 1.1 percentage points. From 1968 to 2007, credit grew, on average, by 4.9 percent a year, while GDP grew by 3.1 percent, a gap of 1.9 percentage points a year.

The difference in growth rates became significantly more pronounced beginning in 1981. From that year until 2007, credit grew on average by 5.7 percent a year, while GDP grew by 3.1 percent. The gap between the two was 2.6 percentage points a year. Therefore, from the early 1980s, it appears that credit was subject to diminishing returns. Credit growth accelerated, but economic growth did not. In large part, this is explained by the U.S. trade deficit which first became pronounced during the early 1980s. The growth in credit did stimulate U.S. demand, but that demand was met by imports and so did not contribute as much to U.S. economic growth as it would have had the United States not imported so much from abroad.

Is it possible that economic growth drove the credit growth instead of credit growth driving the economic growth, as argued throughout this book? That may have been the case in the past under normal conditions, but in recent decades the evidence suggests otherwise. Consider the 1980s. During the five years from the end of 1982 to the end of 1987, credit (adjusted for inflation) expanded by an average of 10.1 percent a year, much more than during any other five-year period since the end of World War II. The gap between credit growth and GDP growth was also particularly wide during those five years, 5.6 percentage points on average. There is absolutely no doubt about what caused the acceleration of credit at that time. It was Reaganomics. The Reagan administration cut taxes and increased military spending. As a result, the annual budget deficit averaged 4.8 percent of GDP over those years, producing a cumulative budget deficit of $976 billion. It was government debt that caused total debt to expand; there is no way to argue that economic growth caused an increase in government debt. It was very clearly the other way around: government debt caused the economy to expand. Government debt powered Reagan's "Morning in

America" economic rebound. This is a lesson that his devotees in the Tea Party need to learn. While Reagan was president, the government debt held by the public increased from $712 billion to $2,052 billion, or by 188 percent. Although the Gipper said that "Government is the problem," he used government debt as the solution.

The second notable period when credit growth greatly outstripped economic growth was the seven years between the end of 2000 and the end of 2007. During those years, credit expanded by an average of 6.4 percent a year while the economy expanded by only 2.4 percent a year on average. The gap between the two was 4.1 percentage points a year.

Government deficits and government debt played a role here, too, but a secondary one. Government debt increased by $1.6 trillion during that period. The GSEs and the issuers of asset-backed securities (ABSs) were in the driver's seat. Their debt expanded by $3.1 trillion and by $2.9 trillion, respectively, during those years. Household sector debt expanded by $6.7 trillion. The question is, did the household sector take the initiative and demand more credit from the GSEs and the ABS issuers, or did Fannie, Freddie, Citi, Countrywide, IndyMac, and the other ABS issuers drive that process? Common sense and the behavioral patterns of the financial industry strongly suggest the financial sector was responsible for stuffing the household sector with debt. That is not to say that the household sector is completely free of blame. Individuals should have behaved more responsibly.

After 1980, there is really no question that credit growth drove economic growth. This truth is underlined by the fact that when the credit could not be repaid and credit therefore ceased to expand, the economy went into crisis. The cause and the effect are clear. Credit growth drove economic growth.

So, Where Does that Leave Us?

Between 1952 and 2007, credit (adjusted for inflation) grew on average by 5 percent a year. Over those years, credit contracted only three times, in 1974, 1975, and 1980. And there were only six years in which credit expanded by only 0 percent to 2 percent. All of these periods corresponded with recession or very weak economic growth. In every instance, however, credit growth reaccelerated a year later or two years later at the most and economic growth recovered. This time, credit growth has not reaccelerated. In 2008, credit expanded 1 percent. In 2009, it was flat. In 2010, it contracted by 1.4 percent. And, during the first half of 2011, it was flat again. These weak numbers are in spite of a $4.6 trillion (90 percent) increase in the U.S. government's debt since the end of 2007 and a $2 trillion increase in the Fed's balance sheet. (The Fed's fiat money creation did not directly contribute to credit growth, but it did have the effect of improving the solvency of the financial sector, which should have facilitated new credit growth.)

No credit growth has meant no economic growth. U.S. economic output has still not returned to the peak it reached in the fourth quarter of 2007. How much longer will this go on? When will credit begin to expand again?

Why Can't TCMD Grow?

The best way to determine when credit will expand again is to consider the prospects for each of the major sectors of the economy separately. Which of those sectors has the capacity and the will to increase its level of debt? (See Exhibit 6.2.)

Household Sector

The household sector is the ultimate end user in every economy. Personal consumption expenditure makes up approximately 70 percent of U.S. GDP. The business sector sells to the household sector; and the financial sector lends to it. Therefore, the financial health of the household sector determines the health of the entire economy. Will this sector take on more debt in the years immediately ahead?

Former Fed Chairman Alan Greenspan wrote about household sector debt in his autobiography, which went to print in June 2007. He began by quoting from an article published in *Fortune* magazine in 1956: "Consumer short-term debt . . . is approaching a historical turning point . . . It must soon adjust itself to the nation's capacity for going in hock, which is not limitless," declared *Fortune* in March 1956. A month later, the magazine added,

EXHIBIT 6.2 Debt by Sector (2010)
$ trillions

	Debt Owed by:	% of Total Debt	% of GDP
Household sector	$13.4	25%	92%
Financial sector	$14.2	27%	98%
Corporate sector	$7.4	14%	51%
Noncorporate businesses	$3.5	7%	24%
Federal government	$9.4	18%	65%
State & local government	$2.6	5%	18%
Miscellaneous others	$2.1	4%	14%
Total credit market debt	$52.6	100%	363%

Source: Federal Reserve, *Flow of Funds Accounts of the United States, second quarter 2011*

"The same general observations apply to mortgage debt—but with double force." Greenspan then added, "Today, nearly fifty years later, the ratio of household debt to income is still rising, and critics are still wringing their hands. In fact, I do not recall a decade free of surges in angst about the mounting debt of households and businesses. Such fears ignore a fundamental fact of modern life: in a market economy, rising debt goes hand in hand with progress."[2]

Exhibit 6.3 puts Greenspan's comments into perspective. It shows household debt as a ratio of household disposable income from 1946 to 2010.

Notice that this ratio had hit 53 percent and was rising rapidly at the time *Fortune* expressed concern about mortgage debt in 1956. Then, from the mid-1960s to the mid-1980s it flattened out around 70 percent. Alan Greenspan became Fed chairman in August 1987. Soon thereafter, household debt relative to disposable income began to rise sharply. That ratio peaked at nearly 140 percent in 2007, just as Greenspan was expounding on the role of rising debt and the facts of life. Unfortunately, American households were incapable of repaying so much debt. They began defaulting on their mortgages in record numbers. The result was a systemic banking crisis and a severe global economic crisis that remains far from over.

One of the facts of life that the chairman seems to have been unaware of is that debt has to be repaid. That means people must earn enough money to repay their debts. Between the time Greenspan became chairman

EXHIBIT 6.3 Ratio of Household Debt to Disposable Personal Income

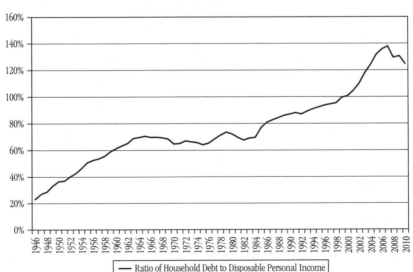

Source: Federal Reserve, *Flow of Funds Accounts of the United States, second quarter 2011,* Table B.100

until 2007, median income in the United States doubled (not adjusted for inflation), but the level of household sector debt increased five and a half times.

Raising debt may go hand in hand with progress so long as it keeps rising; but when it stops rising, progress goes into reverse. Mr. Greenspan believed that property prices would not go down on a nationwide basis. In May 2006, at a Bond Market Association reception, he was quoted as saying the housing "boom is over." But also, "We're not about to go into a situation where prices will go down." And, there is "no evidence home prices are going to collapse." But they did collapse; and they collapsed on a nationwide basis. According to S&P Case-Shiller 20-City Home Price Index, between mid-2006 and mid-2011, they have fallen by 32 percent.

During this crisis, millions of Americans have lost their homes. Moreover, owners' equity as a percentage of household real estate (i.e., the amount of equity homeowners actually have in their homes) has plummeted to a record low. Home prices and homeowners' equity are important because they determine how much collateral the household sector has to borrow against. (See Exhibit 6.4.)

With home values down sharply and equity in homes also down sharply, that means the household sector has much less collateral than before; and that means they will not be able to borrow more. Only higher personal income would enable households to afford additional debt. Median income is declining, however. (See Exhibit 6.5.) And with globalization

EXHIBIT 6.4 Owners' Equity as Percentage of Household Real Estate

Source: Federal Reserve, *Flow of Funds Accounts of the United States, second quarter 2011*

EXHIBIT 6.5 Median U.S. Income, 2010 Dollars

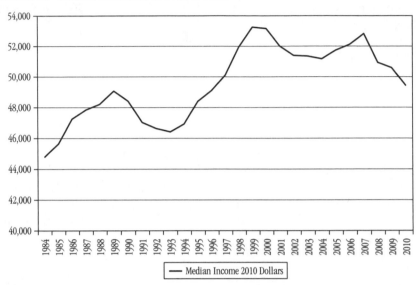

Source: U.S. Census Bureau, Current Population Survey, 2011

exerting downward pressure on U.S. wages, there is no reason for optimism
that personal income will rise significantly any time soon. Add to that the
very high rates of unemployment and it is difficult not to conclude that
the household sector is much more likely to continue reducing its indebtedness than to take it higher again.

It is not at all clear what level of debt to disposable income is sustainable for this sector. If that ratio were to contract back to its pre-Greenspan
level of 70 percent, household debt would contract by $6 trillion and total
credit market debt would shrink by more than 10 percent. The economic
consequences of that would be very harsh.

The Rest of the Private Sector

With the household sector retrenching, it is very unlikely that the rest of
the private sector will expand its level of debt, either.

First consider the financial sector. In the years before the crisis, the
financial sector extended its debt level much more rapidly than any other
sector. The main drivers of credit expansion within the sector were Fannie
Mae and Freddie Mac, followed by the issuers of ABSs (see Chapter 3). How
likely are they to drive credit growth in the years ahead? Fannie and Freddie
were nationalized because their creditors doubted (with good cause) their
solvency and refused to extend them any more credit. Many of the issuers of
ABSs failed and disappeared for the same reason.

Between the end of 2008 and now, with a great deal of help from the government and the Fed, the financial sector has contracted its debt by $3.3 trillion, or by 19 percent to $13.8 trillion at mid-2011. Looking ahead, the sector won't begin to increase its debt level again unless there are viable borrowers in other parts of the economy to which it could extend credit. As previously discussed, demand for new credit from the household sector seems unlikely.

What about the corporate sector? Businesses, too, are unlikely to expand their debt. First, the corporate sector has enough cash and cash flow of its own that it does not need to borrow from the financial sector. And second, with the economy in crisis, the corporate sector has more capacity than it needs already and, therefore, has no intention of investing to build any more. Thus, neither the financial sector nor the corporate sector should be expected to expand their level of debt in the years ahead. (See Exhibit 6.6.)

The Government Sector

That leaves only the government sector.

It was only a $4.6 trillion increase in government debt since the end of 2007 that prevented a contraction in TCMD so sharp that it would have produced a replay of the Great Depression. (See Exhibit 6.7.)

Can the government continue to expand its debt, enabling TCMD (and the economy) to grow? Will it?

EXHIBIT 6.6 Capacity Utilization

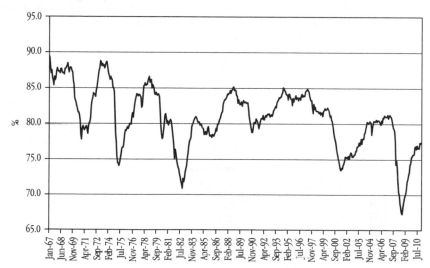

Source: St. Louis Fed

EXHIBIT 6.7 Total Credit Market Debt Actual and if Government Debt Had Remained Flat after 2007

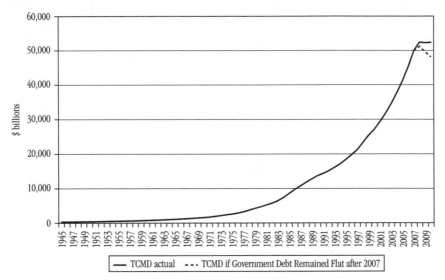

Source: Federal Reserve, *Flow of Funds Accounts of the United States, second quarter 2011*

It could. Total government debt to GDP in the United States is roughly 100 percent. The ratio of government debt held by the public to GDP is approximately 65 percent. The level of Japanese government debt to GDP is around 230 percent. Therefore, there is no financial or economic reason the U.S. government could not increase its level of debt very significantly. However, as will be described in Chapter 7, there are political impediments that may prevent government debt from expanding. If it doesn't, the New Depression will become much worse.

Exhibit 6.8 shows the Congressional Budget Office's estimates for the increase in federal government debt each year out to 2015. The eventual actual numbers could and probably will be very different from these projections. They will be impacted by the actual rate of economic growth, which will affect both tax revenues and government spending; and they may be and probably will be affected by legislative changes made by Congress between now and 2015. Nevertheless, in the following analysis those numbers will be used, for lack of any better alternative.

If we assume that there is no change in the level of debt owed by other sectors—neither an increase nor a decrease—then the growth in TCMD will come solely from the increase in government debt. Is it fair to make that assumption? It could well be far too optimistic about the ability of the private sector to maintain its current level of debt. The household sector has been reducing its debt every quarter since the fourth quarter

EXHIBIT 6.8 Increase in Government Debt Held by the Public as projected by CBO

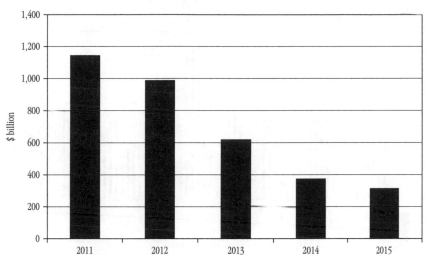

Source: Congressional Budget Office, August 2011

of 2008 and is still very highly geared relative to its disposable income. Moreover, Fannie and Freddie remain in crisis and are likely to reduce their debt level for years to come. As for the issuers of ABSs, it is hard to imagine just how bad the quality of their remaining assets could be, but it seems much more probable that they will continue to shrink their balance sheets rather than expand them in the years ahead. Therefore, to assume that TCMD will increase by as much as government debt increases is an aggressive call. It is more likely that private sector debt will contract and offset the increase in government debt. Nevertheless, in the following paragraphs it will be assumed that private sector debt will remain unchanged.

What impact, then, would the projected increase in government debt have on the overall growth in TCMD and, by extension, on the overall growth of the U.S. economy? Exhibit 6.9 projects out the annual increase in TCMD to 2015. The data are adjusted for inflation to reflect the "real" rate of increase. The rate of inflation is assumed to be 3 percent in 2011 (the average for the first eight months of the year) and 1 percent each year from 2012 to 2015. It could be significantly lower or higher, depending on how much fiat money the Fed creates during those years.

The picture Exhibit 6.9 paints regarding the economy's prospects is a very depressing one. In the past, whenever TCMD has grown at such a slow rate for even one year, the consequences for the economy were harsh and policy makers and/or bankers quickly found a way to ramp up the country's level of debt.

EXHIBIT 6.9 Total Credit Market Debt, Percentage Change, Projected to 2015, adjusted for Inflation

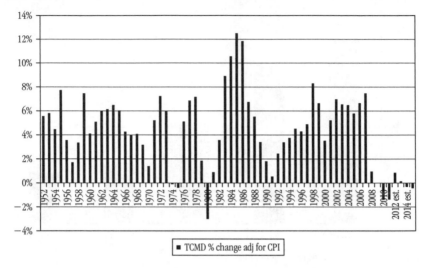

Source: Historic Debt: Fed, Flow of Funds
Historic CPI: St. Louis Fed
Projections: Author

As of the time of writing (November 2011), TCMD has been flat for three years and the economy is into its third year of severe hardship—despite a near doubling of U.S. government debt over that period. If the growth in TCMD remains depressed for the next five years, as the projections above suggest, an economic catastrophe will be unavoidable.

Some commentators have expressed the fear that if things go badly the United States could experience a "lost decade," just as Japan did following the collapse of its credit bubble in 1989.[3] This assessment overlooks the fact that Japan's crisis was mitigated by Japan's ability to export into the booming U.S. and Chinese economies. Domestic demand was depressed but external demand was very strong. During the years immediately ahead, there will be no opportunity for the United States to export its way out of crisis. The global economy will be very depressed. Therefore, the U.S. could experience something far worse than a "lost decade."

The Banking Industry: Why Still Too Big to Fail?

How safe is the U.S. banking sector? FDIC-insured commercial banks held $6,964 billion in domestic deposits at the end of 2010. The largest four banks held 35 percent of that total or $2,436 billion.[4]

Bank of America held $829 billion in deposits (or 11 percent of all domestic deposits), Wells Fargo Bank held $719 billion (10 percent), JPMorgan Chase Bank held $633 billion (9 percent), and Citibank held $255 billion (4 percent). Never before in the history of the United States has there been such a high degree of concentration of the banking sector.

Exhibit 6.10 provides a compressed summary of the balance sheets of these four banks.

Very simply, so long as a bank earns more on its assets than it pays for its liabilities, it is profitable. In the normal course of business, a very small portion of a bank's assets becomes nonperforming and has to be written off as a loss. That generally has only a small negative impact on the bank's profitability. In an economic crisis, however, it is possible that losses on assets become so large that they destroy all the bank's shareholders' equity and then some, in which case the bank fails and its depositors or other creditors do not recover all their assets.

That is what happened in the Great Depression, when 9,000 U.S. banks failed or were merged into other banks. Today, the FDIC insures all the banks' deposits, so when a bank fails, its depositors do not lose their savings. However, if a severe crisis caused a large number of bank deposits to be destroyed, the FDIC would not have sufficient funds to cover the losses and the taxpayers would have to assume responsibility for making good the banks' losses.

As shown in Exhibit 6.10, deposits make up only 44 percent to 45 percent of total liabilities for three of the banks. For Wells Fargo, they account for 67 percent. The remaining liabilities are borrowed from other creditors.

On the assets side of the balance sheet, loans range from 33 percent of total assets (JPMorgan Chase) to 60 percent (Wells Fargo); while trading assets range between 23 percent of total assets at JPMorgan Chase to only 4 percent at Wells Fargo. The remaining assets are composed of other types of investments with varying degrees of risk.

Derivatives add a whole new dimension of risk to the banking system. While the "fair value" of the banks' derivatives positions is recorded in their balance sheets under both assets and liabilities, at times of crisis, those valuations would not adequately capture the counterparty risks inherent in those positions.

In its 2010 consolidated balance sheet, Bank of America recorded $73 billion as *derivative assets* and $55.9 billion as *derivative liabilities,* representing 3.2 percent and 2.7 percent of its assets and liabilities, respectively. However, the notional amount, which "represents the total contract/notional amount of derivative assets and liabilities outstanding," was $68.3 *trillion,* a figure 32 times larger than Bank of America's total assets. In fact, $68 trillion was 8 percent larger than global GDP in 2010.

EXHIBIT 6.10 The Big Four U.S. Banks
2010 Balance Sheet Summary
$ billions

Liabilities	Bank of America		JPMorgan Chase		Citi		Wells Fargo	
	$ billions	% of liab.	$ billions	% of liab.	$ billions	% of liab.	$ billions	% of liab.
Deposits	1,010	45%	930	44%	845	44%	848	67%
Other liabilities	1,027	45%	1,011	48%	903	47%	282	22%
Total liabilities	2,037	90%	1,941	92%	1,748	91%	1,130	90%
Shareholders' equity	228	10%	176	8%	166	9%	128	10%
Total liabilities & shareholders' equity	2,265	100%	2,117	100%	1,914	100%	1,258	100%

Assets	$ billions	% of assets	$ billions	% of assets	$ billions	% of assets	$ billions	% of assets
Loans & leases	940	42%	693	33%	649	34%	757	60%
Trading account	195	9%	490	23%	317	17%	51	4%
Other assets	1,130	50%	934	44%	948	50%	450	36%
Total assets	2,265	100%	2,117	100%	1,914	100%	1,258	100%

Source: 2010 Annual Reports of Bank of America, JPMorgan Chase, Citibank, and Wells Fargo

In normal business conditions, the notional amounts, representing the total contract amount, are not so important as they are netted out against other positions and generally do not represent the value at risk. However, in times of crisis, as in 2008 when major institutions (i.e., the counterparties to those trades) were failing or close to collapse, the risk of being exposed to trillions of dollars worth of derivatives contracts increased dramatically.

Exhibit 6.11 shows just how great some U.S. banks' exposure to the derivatives market actually is.

In 2010, JPM Chase recorded "total derivatives notional amounts" exposure of $78.9 trillion; Bank of America, $68.3 trillion, and Citigroup, $47.5 trillion. Combined, that came to $194.7 trillion for those three banks alone. Compare that amount with global GDP (i.e., the annual economic output of the world) of $63 trillion in 2010. It was more than three times larger.

At the end of 2010, worldwide total notional amount of derivatives contracts was $669 trillion. Those three U.S. banks accounted for 29 percent of that global total.

Almost 90 percent of the worldwide total, or approximately $600 trillion, was composed of over-the-counter (OTC) transactions, which are subject to limited regulation and provide very little transparency. Only 10 percent trade through exchanges. One of the most important sections of Dodd–Frank, the banking sector reform act that was signed into law in July 2010, required that most OTC derivatives be traded on an exchange (rather than OTC) by July 2011. That did not happen, however. The implementation of that part of Dodd–Frank has been pushed back to an unspecified date.

Consequently, there is no greater transparency or oversight of this $600 trillion OTC can of worms than before the crisis began. Exchange trading would have provided transparency as to who undertook the trades and perhaps shed light on the rationale behind the transactions. There is a very real possibility that such transparency would have exposed fraud, manipulation, and accounting trickery on a very large scale. One thing is certain: $669 trillion of transactions is too large an amount to have been entered into for hedging purposes alone. It is equivalent to roughly $100,000 per person on earth—or, more or less, the value of everything produced on this planet during the last 20 years combined. There simply aren't $669 trillion worth of things in the world to hedge.

It may be that sometime after Dodd–Frank passed, regulators realized they did not want to see (and that the economy could not bear to see) the things that greater transparency would expose. The exposure of large losses or widespread unethical activity could set off a new phase of the systemic crisis and inflict even greater damage on the economy than anything experienced thus far.

Daylight is said to be the best antiseptic. In this case, however, the danger is that daylight may expose gangrene.

EXHIBIT 6.11 Notional Amount of Derivative Contracts
as of December 31, 2010
$ billions

	JPMorgan Chase & Co.	Bank of America	Citigroup Inc.
Interest rate contracts			
Swaps	46,299	42,719	27,084
Futures and forwards	9,298	9,939	4,874
Written options	4,075	2,888	3,431
Purchased options	3,968	3,026	3,306
Total Interest Rate Contracts	**63,640**	**58,572**	**38,695**
Credit Derivatives	**5,472**	**4,319**	**2,512**
Foreign Exchange Contracts			
Cross-currency swaps	2,568	630	1,119
Spot, futures and forwards	3,893	2,653	2,746
Written options	674	440	599
Purchased options	649	417	536
Total Foreign Exchange Contracts	**7,784**	**4,140**	**5,000**
Equity Contracts			
Swaps	116	42	68
Futures and forwards	49	79	20
Written options	430	243	492
Purchased options	377	193	474
Total Equity Contracts	**972**	**557**	**1,054**
Commodity Contracts			
Swaps	349	90	19
Spot, futures and forwards	170	414	116
Written options	264	86	61
Purchased optons	254	85	62
Total Commodity Contracts	**1,037**	**675**	**258**
Total Derivative Notional Amounts	**78,905**	**68,263**	**47,519**

Three banks	Global GDP	3 banks to Global GDP
$194,687	**$63,049**	**3.1**

Note: The data for Citigroup shows "Trading derivatives" only. Another $288 billion in Hedging Instruments and $294 billion in "Other derivative instruments" are not included above.
Source: 2010 Annual Reports of JPMorgan Chase, Bank of America, and Citigroup Inc.

It is unclear how much damage would be caused by the bankruptcy of a financial institution with a derivatives exposure equivalent to one year's worth of global economic output. It can only be imagined that the damage would range between catastrophic and cataclysmic. That is what is meant by *too big to fail.*

Regarding their size, there is another possibility that warrants consideration. Banks may have been allowed to remain too big to fail because they are too bankrupt to split apart. Due to the size and opacity of the derivatives market, there is at least some risk that the sum of the banks' parts could add up to a multitrillion dollar negative number. Were that the case, it would explain why the government did not nationalize at least some banks when injecting large amounts of capital into the financial system in 2009: it had no desire to consolidate massive bank losses onto its own balance sheet.

The same theory might explain why Fannie and Freddie were put into "conservatorship" instead of being nationalized: the government may simply be unwilling to bear the responsibility for all the losses from Fannie and Freddie that might eventually come to light. Conservatorship status leaves open the possibility that the losses will yet be borne by creditors and counterparties rather than the government and the taxpayers.

The concentration of the banking sector and the continuing inadequacy of its regulation pose a grave threat to the U.S. economy. The fact is, however, in a world where credit growth drives economic growth, the economy is held hostage by the banking industry.

Any regulatory action that damages the interest of the banks—regardless of how justified—has the potential to inflict significant, even fatal, harm on the economy. Until these conflicts are resolved, the banking industry will continue to be a dangerously destabilizing factor within the U.S. economy.

Global Imbalances: Still Unresolved

In the post–Bretton Woods era, trade liberalization, cross-border capital flows, and currency manipulation combined to produce widespread global imbalances that have destabilized the world economy. In the past, trade between nations had to balance because deficits had to be paid for with gold. Since 1971, however, it has become possible to finance large trade deficits with debt denominated in fiat money. As a result, debt-financed trade generated decades of rapid global economic growth as the countries with trade surpluses lent money to the countries with trade deficits to allow them to consume and import more from one year to the next. Debt-financed trade worked beautifully until 2008, when the debtors in the trade-deficit countries became incapable of repaying their debts. Then the crisis began.

These global imbalances have not been corrected. On one side are the trade surplus countries such as China, Germany, and the oil exporters, who cannot consume as much as they produce. On the other side are the trade deficit countries such as the United States, the United Kingdom, Greece, Ireland, and Spain, who cannot produce as much as they consume. Moreover, the trade deficit countries can no longer afford to consume as much as they did in the past because they can't repay their past debts. Forced austerity in the deficit countries leaves the surplus countries with excess industrial capacity, which means there is no reason for them to invest more. Without further investment or export growth, their economies cannot grow. At the same time, in many cases, the inability of the deficit countries to repay their debts means that the surplus countries cannot recover the loans they made to those countries. In Europe, the difficulty of deficit countries to repay their loans is threatening the solvency of the banks in the surplus countries that extended those loans. (See Exhibit 6.12.)

EXHIBIT 6.12 Global Imbalances
Current Account Balances
Selected Countries, 2010

Surplus Countries	US$ billions	% of GDP
China	305	5.2
Japan	196	3.6
Germany	187	5.7
Russia	71	4.8
Saudi Arabia	67	14.9
Netherlands	56	7.1
Singapore	49	22.2
Taiwan	40	9.3
Kuwait	37	27.8
Hong Kong	14	6.2
Deficit Countries	**US$ billions**	**% of GDP**
United States	471	3.2
United Kingdom	72	3.2
Italy	68	3.3
Spain	64	4.6
India	43	2.6
Greece	32	10.4
Portugal	23	9.9

Source: IMF, Word Economic Database, September 2011

As long as debt in the trade deficit countries continued to increase, their demand for imports grew and global investment and industrial capacity expanded to fill that demand. Now that the debtors can bear no more debt, the global growth paradigm no longer works. Not only is there no new demand to justify new investment, there is less demand than before, resulting in a tremendous amount of unused industrial capacity around the world.

The United States bears the greatest responsibility for allowing the global imbalances to develop. First, President Richard Nixon destroyed the Bretton Woods international monetary system, which had been designed to ensure that international trade did balance. Later, the United States promoted trade liberalization and cross-border capital flows with no concern for the very large U.S. trade deficits that emerged as a result. Finally, it failed to act when many of its trading partners blatantly manipulated the value of their currencies in a way that prevented the trade imbalances from correcting.

When the U.S. credit bubble began in earnest in the 1980s, other countries expanded their industrial capacity to satisfy the United States' rapidly expanding debt-financed demand. The United States began to deindustrialize and wage rates stagnated, but that did not matter so long as U.S. stock prices and home prices kept inflating, because American households were able to borrow more and to consume more. The United States was able to import more each year, and that demand absorbed the rest of the world's rapidly increasing industrial supply.

In the developing world where the most rapid economic expansion took place, wage rates were (and remain) far too low to allow domestic demand to absorb the supply of goods being produced in those countries. In countries like China, for instance, where 80 percent of the population earns less than $10 per day, the factory workers cannot afford to buy the things they make in the factories where they work.

That was not a problem, however, so long as U.S. households borrowed and consumed more every year. It is a very grave problem now, however, that that paradigm of debt-financed demand has reached the maximum extent of its potential and has begun to go into reverse.

Where now will China and a dozen other countries that had grown through export-led growth sell the goods they cannot afford to buy themselves? Will they continue to invest aggressively, building yet more industrial capacity? What will become of the excess industrial capacity now in place? What of the workforce there employed? What of the bank loans that financed the industrial capacity? Disastrously, they won't sell them. They won't build more. It won't be used. They'll lose their jobs. They won't be repaid, and the banks will fail unless they are bailed out by their governments.

Finally, as for the U.S. economy, it is no longer viable the way it is currently structured. The country is deindustrializing because wage rates in the U.S. manufacturing sector are 30 to 40 times higher than the prevailing global wage rate for factory workers, which is $5 per day. Consequently, the nature of the economy has changed. An economic paradigm built on debt expansion, asset price bubbles, and the service industry replaced the previous paradigm that was centered on the production of tangible goods. In 2008, however, that new paradigm exhausted its potential to support asset prices or the demand for services, leaving the country deindustrialized and without the kind of capital structure capable of generating profits, savings, and new investments. That left the United States ripe for a brutal economic contraction.

The crisis has caused the process of deindustrialization to accelerate. More than two million manufacturing jobs (or 15 percent of the total) have been lost since the end of 2007. Nearly a third of all U.S. manufacturing jobs have disappeared over the last ten years. The U.S. current account deficit corrected from $800 billion in 2006 to $377 billion in 2009, but it has widened sharply again since then, reaching $471 billion in 2010. The currency manipulation that perpetuates the U.S. trade disadvantage has intensified since the crisis began as reflected in the $3 trillion (40 percent) increase in total foreign exchange reserves since the end of 2008.

In other words, there has been no adjustment to the global imbalances that played a leading role in creating this economic disaster. The elimination of those imbalances is inevitable, and it still lies ahead.

Looking ahead, the rest of the world won't buy more from the United States. It will buy less. When the United States buys less from other countries, other countries have fewer dollars and so will buy less from the United States. That was one of the lessons from 2001 when the stock market bubble popped and from 2008 when the housing bubble popped. External factors will exacerbate the depression in the United States during the years ahead, not ameliorate it.

Vision and Leadership Are Still Lacking

The adoption of fiat money permitted the abuse of Keynesian stimulus on a scale that would have horrified John Maynard Keynes, and it opened up possibilities for credit expansion that earlier generations of economists would not have dreamt possible. What wrongly passed as free-market ideology (in a free market, the government does not create money and manipulate interest rates) allowed the financial industry to completely transform our world with financial leverage. Now, however, that economic paradigm of debt-driven growth is played out. The private sector cannot bear any additional debt and the crisis that the retrenchment of the private sector has created has begun to infect governments around the world. The end of growth has collapsed tax revenues but driven government spending higher and produced a sovereign debt crisis around the periphery of Europe that not only threatens to spread to the core but also portends what awaits most of the rest of the world over the next decade.

Policy makers—many of whom were responsible for encouraging the proliferation of credit—act surprised that the global economy has not rebound from the crisis that began in 2008. They should not be. It has been obvious for a long time that a global boom driven by surging fiat money–denominated credit would ultimately end disastrously.

Keynes quipped that in the long run we are all dead. But must the long run arrive today? Where are the visionaries with brilliant ideas that will postpone that day of reckoning, push it back for a few more years, for a decade or—dare we hope—actually generate a plan that cheats fate by devising a strategy to allow us to use the resources at our disposal to invest our way back to solvency?

The business community has put forward no bold initiatives. The Republicans—after having expanded the national debt by 188 percent under President Ronald Reagan and 77 percent more under President George W. Bush—have recently found their old-time religion and are determined to cut government spending now—at a time when only government spending is keeping the economy afloat. The Democrats have no discernible ideas at all. President Barack Obama relied too heavily on the advice of many of those responsible for causing the crisis and has no contingency plan to implement now that the second down leg of the collapse has begun.

Finally, the Libertarians are actively promoting policies sure to bring about immediate economic hell, in the faith that punishment and suffering are the prerequisites to an economic afterlife in a better world. While in the end their philosophy of economic karma may ultimately prove correct, before accepting the remedy of recovery through collapse, other approaches should be put to the test. Economic reincarnation could take much longer than the Libertarians anticipate. The Renaissance did follow the fall of Rome—but only after ten centuries.

Tragically, no new ideas are being seriously considered in the public arena. Therefore, it is necessary to consider next how this New Depression will play out.

Notes

1. Irving Fisher, *The Purchasing Power of Money: Its Determination and Relation to Credit, Interest and Crises* (New York: The Macmillan Company, 1912), p. 131.
2. Alan Greenspan, *The Age of Turbulence* (New York: The Penguin Press, 2007), p. 346.
3. Actually two lost decades so far.
4. The data for individual banks are as of June 30, 2010, and so are not exactly comparable to the figure for total deposits, which is for the end of 2010. Nevertheless, the data are a good approximation.

CHAPTER 7

How It Plays Out

Requiring a central bank to print money to increase government's purchasing power invariably ignites a hyperinflationary firestorm. The result through history has been toppled governments and severe threats to societal stability.

—Alan Greenspan[1]

Visualize a sinking ship with captain and crew frantically bailing out water to keep the ship above the waves. Now, instead of a great wooden vessel, imagine a credit-inflated rubber raft from which credit is leaking through numerous holes. Policy makers are desperately pumping more credit into the raft to stop it from going down. That raft is the global economy. Humanity lives on top of it. There are no lifeboats. If the raft sinks, people are going to die.

That harsh reality is driving and will continue to drive economic policy.

The prospects for rescue are far from certain, and, in fact, diminishing with each passing month. Nevertheless, policy makers can be counted on to keep pumping credit into that raft until their strength runs out. They are lost at sea and don't know what else they can do.

The Business Cycle

Although economists disagree on many subjects, there are three things they do agree on. First, it is clear that economic output has risen sharply (but not steadily) since the Industrial Revolution began in the late eighteenth century. Second, it is agreed that an economy tends to move toward a state of general equilibrium in which prices adjust until supply meets demand. The French economist Leon Walras (1834–1910) developed the theory of general equilibrium during the 1870s. Finally, economists agree that the tendency toward equilibrium is disrupted by *business cycles*—periods of unusual prosperity (booms) followed by periods of economic depression (or busts).

There is widespread disagreement, however, about the causes of the business cycle. Wesley Mitchell (1874–1948), Columbia University professor and director of research at the National Bureau of Economic Research, did perhaps more than any other economist to develop a comprehensive understanding of the phenomena or, as he put it, to explain "the interrelations among cyclical fluctuations in the production of raw materials, industrial equipment and consumers' goods; in the volume of savings and investments; in the promotion of new enterprises, in banking, in the disbursement of incomes to individuals and the spending of incomes, in prices, costs, profits and the emotional aberrations of business judgments."[2] Mitchell provided a useful and interesting overview of many of the most well known business cycle theories in the first chapter of his book, *Business Cycles: The Problem and Its Setting*, which was published in 1927. He grouped them under ten categories:

1. **The Weather.** Here weather patterns and sunspots are held to affect agricultural prices and, thereby, the broader economy.
2. **Uncertainty.** The business community tends to misjudge future demand and overproduces or underproduces as a result. The need to adjust output to actual demand then sets off the cycle.
3. **The Emotional Factor in Business Decisions.** Mood swings within the business community between excessive optimism and excessive pessimism is thought responsible for the booms and busts of investment.
4. **Innovation, Promotion, Progress.** This theory states that innovations and waves of innovations cause changes in both the supply and demand for products to which the economy must adjust.
5. **The Process of Saving and Investment.** One version of this theory blames the business cycle on a scarcity of capital, while another attributes it to oversaving.
6. **Construction Work.** This theory contends that booms and depressions originate in the construction industry and spread out to the rest of the economy.
7. **General Overproduction.** Investment by the business community sets off a period of prosperity, but then carries on for too long until there is excess production that can't be sold. At that point, investment is reduced, resulting in the depression.
8. **Banking Operations.** Credit expansion causes the boom, but the boom goes into reverse when credit ceases to expand.
9. **Production and the Flow of Money Incomes.** Production expands faster than wages, eventually leading to unsold goods, falling prices, and depression.

10. **The Role Played by Profit-Making.** "The distinguishing characteristic of the(se) theories . . . is that they represent the alternatives of prosperity and depression as arising from profit-making itself."[3]

These are all interesting ideas, and many of them overlap in a variety of ways. All of them are worth considering. There is at least one thing all cycles have in common, however: credit. Ludwig von Mises pointed this out in the following astute observation:

> *In fact, every nonmonetary trade-cycle doctrine tacitly assumes—or ought to assume—that credit expansion is an attendant phenomenon of the boom. It cannot help admitting that in the absence of such a credit expansion no boom could emerge and that the increase in the supply of money (in the broader sense) is a necessary condition of the general upward movement of prices.[4]*

That statement is correct. Booms do not occur in the absence of credit expansion. It is the theme of this book that the adoption of fiat money in place of commodity money, combined with regulatory changes that reduced banks' liquidity reserves, allowed an unprecedented explosion of credit, which, in turn, generated an equally extraordinary economic boom. Mitchell would have rightly included this theory under the category of "Banking Operation." Fiat money could also be thought of as an innovation in the Schumpeterian sense, however.[5] Therefore, this theory could also be included under the fourth category on Mitchell's list, "Innovation, Promotion, Progress."

Debt: Public and Private

How things play out will depend on whether credit expands or contracts in the years ahead. That is because the boom gives way to the depression when credit stops expanding. To quote von Mises again, ". . . a credit-expansion boom must unavoidably lead to a process which everyday speech calls the depression." Von Mises said:

> *As soon as the afflux of additional fiduciary media comes to an end, the airy castle of the boom collapses. The entrepreneurs must restrict their activities because they lack the funds for their continuation on the exaggerated scale. Prices drop suddenly because these distressed firms try to obtain cash by throwing inventories on the market dirt cheap. Factories are closed, the continuation of construction projects in progress is halted, workers are discharged.[6]*

That was true not only in the Great Depression, but also in all the severe economic crises that have broken out during the decades following the collapse of Bretton Woods: the Latin American debt crisis of the early 1980s, the Japanese crisis that began in 1990, the Mexican peso crisis of 1994, the Asian crisis of 1997, and the Russian crisis of 1998. When the credit stopped expanding, the depression began.

The current crisis in the United States is no different; when credit ceased to expand, the depression began. This depression, however, has not been allowed to run its course. During the Great Depression, unimpeded market forces purged the economy of the credit-driven excesses of the Roaring Twenties. That left economic output in 1933 at roughly half the level it had reached in 1929. This time, the government has intervened aggressively to prevent a similar outcome. Private sector debt in the United States began contracting in the fourth quarter of 2008. Between then and mid-2011, it contracted by $3.4 trillion. Government debt expanded by $3.9 trillion, however, to offset that contraction. As a result, total credit has grown, but by less than 1 percent over those 11 quarters (and it is still below the peak it reached in the first quarter of 2009). The lack of meaningful credit growth has thrown the economy into crisis. The expansion of government debt, however, has at least prevented the economy from collapsing into a new Great Depression.

It is important to understand that the increase in government debt did more than just offset the contraction in private sector debt. Had government debt not increased by so much, the economic crisis would have been far worse and, consequently, private sector debt would have shrunk by far more.

In 2009, private sector debt contracted by $1.5 trillion, while government debt expanded by $1.4 trillion. In 2010, private sector debt contracted by $1.4 trillion, while government debt expanded by $1.6 trillion. During the first half of 2011, on an annualized basis, private sector debt contracted by $586 billion and government debt expanded by $760 billion. Furthermore, the adjustment that has taken place was facilitated by the creation of $2 trillion in fiat money by the Fed, which tripled the size of the central bank's balance sheet during those two and a half years.

It is not at all certain how much further private sector debt must contract before it reaches a sustainable level. As described in Chapter 6, the household sector, the key sector within the economy, remains very heavily indebted relative to past standards. Meanwhile the median income in the country is falling—in large part due to the ongoing competitive pressures stemming from globalization. Therefore, there is every reason to fear that the process of deleveraging by the private sector has much further to run.

EXHIBIT 7.1 Change in Government Debt and Private Sector Debt, Quarter on Quarter

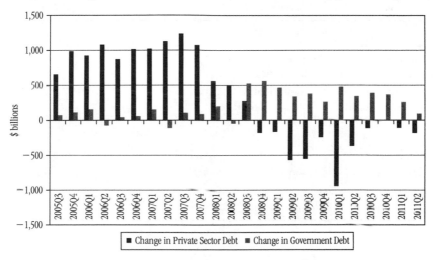

Source: Federal Reserve, *Flow of Funds Accounts of the United States, second quarter 2011*

How things play out from here will depend on whether the government continues increasing its debt enough to prevent credit, and therefore the economy, from collapsing. (See Exhibit 7.1.)

2011: The Starting Point

Credit growth, inflation, and fiat money creation will determine the fate of the U.S. economy over the years immediately ahead. Exhibit 7.2 provides a snapshot of how those factors changed during 2011. The year-end numbers are estimates based on trends during the first nine months of the year.

There was $52.4 trillion in TCMD outstanding at the beginning of 2011. It is estimated to increase by 1.6 percent to $53.3 trillion by the year-end. Private sector debt contracted by $293 billion during the first half and is assumed to remain unchanged during the second half. The estimate for the increase in government debt is based on the projections of the Congressional Budget Office.

The inflation rate is estimated to be 3 percent, the average rate of consumer price inflation during the first eight months of the year. TCMD growth is adjusted for inflation by deducting the inflation rate from the TCMD growth number. Inflation-adjusted TCMD is estimated to contract by 1.4 percent for the full year.

The assets of the Federal Reserve are estimated to be $2.9 trillion at the end of the year, a $500 billion increase from the end of 2010.

EXHIBIT 7.2 2011: The Starting Point
$ billions

	2011 est.
TCMD beginning of the year	52,399
Change in government debt (CBO estimate)	1,145
Change in private sector debt (first half actual in 2011)	−293
Change in TCMD	852
TCMD end of the year	53,251
TCMD growth	1.6%
CPI estimate	3.0%
TCMD adjusted for inflation	−1.4%
Federal Reserve assets	2,900
Fiat money creation during the year	500

2012: Expect QE3

What should be expected for 2012?

Politics will have a greater impact on the economy than normal because of the presidential elections in November. At the start of the year, the economy is likely to be in recession or close to recession because of the weak credit growth during 2011. The household sector and the financial sector will remain crippled by overindebtedness and the stimulus provided in recent years by the government sector will be fading.

A large new government spending program could create jobs and boost economic growth, but that will not happen. The Republican Party has the majority in the House of Representatives and has vowed to block any additional fiscal stimulus. Many Republican members of Congress oppose government spending on ideological grounds. All of them understand that a weak economy and high unemployment will increase the chances of a Republican candidate being elected president in November 2012. Therefore, it is very unlikely that the House will pass any government spending measures that would improve the short-term economic outlook before then. The possibility of any additional fiscal stimulus before 2013 seems next to impossible for that reason.

Consequently, government debt will increase by no more than the current CBO projection of $989 billion. Assuming again that private sector debt remains unchanged, TCMD would increase by the same amount. In that case, TCMD would increase by 1.9 percent during the year. Inflation adjusted TCMD would therefore contract by 1.1 percent, assuming an inflation rate of 3 percent. (See Exhibit 7.3.)

EXHIBIT 7.3 2012: The Year of Dangerous Politics
$ billions

	2011 est.	2012 est.
TCMD beginning of the year	52,399	53,251
Change in government debt (CBO estimate)	1,145	989
Change in private sector debt (first half actual in 2011)	−293	0
Change in TCMD	852	989
TCMD end of the year	53,251	54,240
TCMD growth	1.6%	1.9%
CPI estimate	3.0%	3.0%
TCMD adjusted for inflation	−1.4%	−1.1%
Federal Reserve assets	2,900	3,900
Fiat money creation during the year	500	1,000

That leaves only monetary stimulus to prop up the economy; and, as the Federal Funds rate (the interest rate the Fed directly controls) is already very close to 0 percent, monetary policy means more fiat money creation. Fed Chairman Ben Bernanke and the other decision makers who shape Fed policy are fully aware of how close the global economy is to collapsing into severe depression. They also realize that, with fiscal policy blocked, only they have the power to prevent that outcome. They will not hesitate to use that power—and to use it forcefully.

Quantitative easing (QE) works best when combined with fiscal stimulus, as Bernanke explained in November 2002.[7] Forced to act alone, the Fed will have to be aggressive. With the economy in or near recession, the inflationary pressures of mid-2011 will have abated. That will allow the Fed to begin printing more money. The Fed's strategy will be to push up the stock market in order to "create wealth" and fuel consumption and economic output. Therefore, QE3 will have to be large enough to inspire a shock and awe effect that drives stock prices higher. The challenge for the Fed will be to print enough money to hold up the economy without printing so much that it generates high rates of inflation. The Fed cannot afford to let the money supply (i.e., the credit supply) contract. To ensure that it doesn't, it will print as many dollars as it takes. However, it will do its best to strike the right balance between printing enough money to hold up the economy without printing so much that it loses control over inflation. In this balancing act, it will be helped by the strong deflationary pressure in the global economy that stems from extreme excess industrial capacity around the world. In this scenario, it will be assumed that the Fed prints an additional $1 trillion before the presidential oath of office is taken on January 20, 2013.

That would increase the Fed's balance sheet by $1 trillion to $3.9 trillion.

Impact on Asset Prices

How would asset prices respond? In this scenario, stock prices would move significantly higher from the time that QE3 is announced. Gold and silver would spike higher. The price of food and other commodities would also jump. Bond yields would be kept low (effectively set) by Fed purchases of government bonds. The dollar would fall relative to other currencies, as faith in the reserve currency status of the dollar continued to erode.

QE3 would prevent the economy from collapsing into a severe depression by pushing up stock prices. Higher stock prices would create a positive wealth effect that would give a short-term boost to the economy. The recovery, however, would be short-lived because inflation (caused by rapidly rising commodity prices) would accelerate after a lag of six months or so. Rising prices would undermine "real" (inflation-adjusted) GDP growth. Overall, the economy may grow by 1.0 percent during 2012, while unemployment remained at elevated levels above 8 percent.

Then, the efficacy of QE3 would begin to fade as inflation accelerated toward the end of the year. The economy would begin to move back into recession around the time of the presidential inauguration.

Thus, more fiat money creation is likely to prevent economic collapse in 2012. Fiscal stimulus will be required for the economy to make it through the following two years, however. What form that fiscal stimulus takes and, for that matter, whether the economy receives any fiscal stimulus at all, will depend on who then controls Congress and the presidency.

2013–2014: Three Scenarios

After the presidential and congressional elections in November 2012, the political environment may have changed radically or it may not have changed at all. Republicans may be in complete political control, the Democrats may be, or control may continue to be divided. One or both parties may have reconsidered their positions on the role of the government and the wisdom of government spending by the time 2013 begins. Numerous political and ideological scenarios are imaginable. In the end, however, the course pursued by policy makers is likely to follow one of three paths:

1. The government provides no additional stimulus, either fiscal or monetary.
2. The government does not provide any additional fiscal stimulus, but the Fed supplies QE on a very much larger scale in order to compensate for the shortage of fiscal stimulus.
3. The government provides a new large round of fiscal stimulus.

The impact of each of these scenarios will be considered in turn.

Scenario One: No More Stimulus, Either Fiscal or Monetary

The latest projections from the Congressional Budget Office suggest the government's budget deficit will shrink from $1,284 billion in 2011 to $973 billion in 2012, $510 billion in 2013, and $265 billion in 2014. When a government spends less from one year to the next, that reduction in spending acts as a drag on the economy. If those projections materialize, then the $311 billion reduction in the government deficit in 2012 will deduct 2 percent from GDP, the $463 billion reduction in 2013 will deduct 2.8 percent from GDP, and the $245 billion reduction in 2014 will deduct 1.4 percent from GDP. That would create a very difficult economic environment. Consequently, it is likely that the contraction of private sector debt would accelerate, largely because bankruptcies and defaults would increase.

In the absence of any additional stimulus of any kind, the contraction in TCMD would set off a downward spiral in the economy. Asset prices would fall and business losses would mount, each exacerbating the other. Unemployment would begin to climb higher. A new round of consumer defaults and corporate bankruptcies would begin. Nonperforming assets would proliferate throughout the financial sector and, so, banks would begin to fail. In the absence of new government intervention—say, on the scale of TARP—a systemic crisis would quickly envelop the banking system and, within a week of the first major bank failure, most of the savings of the country (deposits, money market funds, mutual fund investments) would be destroyed. Credit cards would no longer be accepted. Automatic teller machines would not work. By then the stock market would have fallen by 90 percent or more.

Luckily, as humans have evolved with a very strong survival instinct, this scenario of near-term economic suicide is almost certain not to occur. Chapter 8, Disaster Scenarios, describes what should be expected if it does.

Scenario Two: QE Only

As in Scenario One, in the absence of additional fiscal stimulus, the economy would begin to weaken early in 2013. Unemployment would rise, while consumption, profits, investment, and the stock market would fall. To stave off a severe depression death-spiral, the Fed would flip the overdrive switch on the printing presses and create something on the order of $3 trillion more in both 2013 and 2014. That would take the central bank's balance sheet up from $3.9 trillion at the end of 2012 to $9.9 trillion at the end of 2014. The new money would push up the stock market if deployed aggressively enough. If necessary, the Fed would begin to buy stocks directly just as it is buying bonds now. The Bank of Japan has done that, and the Fed would too, if push comes to shove.

That would create more wealth, particularly among the wealthy, but the dollar would lose a great deal of its remaining value. Food and other commodity prices would double or triple and even core inflation would surge toward 8 percent, if not double-digits. Inflation-adjusted TCMD and GDP would contract sharply and unemployment would jump toward 15 percent.

Should this policy persist so long, the November 2014 congressional elections would produce a political revolution, most likely involving a protectionist uprising that puts an end to globalization. Gold could easily top $5,000 an ounce by then. Severe stagnation would prevail.

Scenario Three: Massive Fiscal Stimulus

This is the most probable scenario.

When confronted with the choice, people will almost always choose to die tomorrow rather than to die today. For that reason, it is very likely that U.S. policy makers will choose to apply a great deal of new fiscal stimulus to the economy during 2013 and 2014 (and beyond) rather than allowing the catastrophic collapse of the global economy that would otherwise occur.

In this scenario, it is assumed that the government will run budget deficits of $1.9 trillion in both 2013 and 2014; and that the economy will expand by 2 percent in both years as a result. Economies are like bicycles—they either move forward or they fall over. Two percent growth is close to the minimum necessary to prevent the U.S. economy from falling over. The following paragraphs explain how these projections for the government's deficits are derived.

Credit growth has driven economic growth in the United States for decades. So how much credit growth would be required to generate real (i.e., inflation-adjusted) growth of 2 percent during 2013 and 2014? To answer that question, it is first necessary to estimate what the inflation rate will be. Here, it is assumed that inflation will be 4 percent in both years.

What the actual inflation rate turns out to be will be determined, in large part, by how much fiat money the Fed creates each year. The more money the Fed creates, the higher the inflation rate will be. However, there will also be very strong countervailing deflationary pressures because, in most industries, global supply greatly exceeds global demand. That is because wage growth has not kept pace with the increase in production.

How much money the Fed prints during 2013 and 2014 will be determined by how much of the government's budget deficit the private sector is willing to finance at low interest rates. The Fed will have to monetize the shortfall. This question cannot be answered with any degree of certainty.

However, one of the lessons that should be understood from the economic crisis in Japan is that when big economic bubbles pop, the private sector has nowhere safe to invest all the money that it made during the bubble years. Therefore, the private sector is happy to invest that money (as well as its large annual cash flow) into government bonds even at very low interest rates. That explains why the Japanese government has been able to increase its level of debt relative to GDP from 60 percent when the crisis began in 1990 to approximately 230 percent at the end of 2011, while the interest rate it pays to borrow money for 10 years is still only around 1 percent a year.

Similar credit market conditions will exist in the United States' post-bubble world during the years ahead. The private sector will be glad to invest the money it made during the bubble—and also its large annual cash flow—into U.S. government bonds even at a low interest rate because there won't be anywhere else to safely invest that money.

Still, in this scenario, the size of the government's budget deficits is so large that private sector purchases probably won't be enough to finance them without pushing the interest rates on government bonds to a much higher level. High interest rates would damage the economy. Therefore, the Fed is likely to have to monetize a significant amount of the government's debt during 2013 and 2014 to keep interest rates from rising.

In this scenario, then, it is assumed that the Fed will print enough new fiat money to finance half of the government's budget deficit in 2013 and 2014. It is also assumed that this will result in an inflation rate of 4 percent. Fiat money creation will push commodity prices up, but globalization will push almost all other consumer goods prices down.

Given an inflation rate of 4 percent, the economy will have to grow by 6 percent in nominal terms to achieve 2 percent growth in real terms. At the end of 2012, the size of U.S. GDP is expected to be $15.7 trillion. To grow by 2 percent in real terms would require the economy to expand in nominal terms by $942 billion in 2013 and by $961 billion in 2014.

Since credit growth drives economic growth, the next question is how much credit would have to expand in those years in order to generate that much nominal economic growth. As explained earlier, on average from 1952 to 2007, inflation-adjusted credit expanded by 5.0 percent a year, while real GDP expanded by 3.3 percent a year. The ratio of GDP growth to credit growth was thus 66.4 percent over that period. That ratio has been declining over time; more and more credit has been required to generate economic growth. Between 1981 and 2007, that ratio was 54.5 percent. And between 2001 and 2007, it was only 35.8 percent. This suggests there has been a diminishing return on credit. And, it suggests that a growing amount of credit has been misallocated.

Fifty percent is roughly the midpoint between the average for the last 50 years and the figure for the most recent period, 2001 to 2007, when credit misallocation was particularly bad. So, a ratio of 50 percent economic growth to credit growth will be used to calculate how much credit growth will be required in 2013 and 2014 if the economy is to grow by 2 percent each year. In other words, it is assumed that $2 of credit growth will be required to generate $1 of GDP growth. To generate $942 billion in nominal economic growth in 2013 will take twice as much credit growth, $1,884 billion. And, to generate $961 billion in nominal economic growth in 2014 will require $1,922 billion in credit growth.

The final assumption is that private sector debt will remain unchanged in both years. Two percent economic growth should be enough to prevent a debt deflation downward spiral; however, it is unlikely to be enough to cause the private sector to significantly increase its level of borrowing. Therefore, it is assumed that all the increase in TCMD will come about as the result of an increase in the government's debt. Put differently, the government will have to run a budget deficit of $1,884 billion in 2013 and $1,922 billion in 2014. That would be equivalent to 11.8 percent of GDP in both years. The highest budget deficit thus far in this crisis was 10 percent of GDP in 2010. The increase in government expenditure could come about either due to increased domestic spending or as the result of a war.

Under these assumptions, government debt would amount to 81 percent of GDP at the end of 2013 and 92 percent at the end of 2014. The Fed would create $942 billion in 2013 and $961 billion in 2014 to finance half of the government's budget deficits during those years. The balance sheet of the central bank would grow to $5.8 trillion by the end of 2014.

Exhibit 7.4 summarizes the projected changes in GDP, inflation, and credit as projected in this scenario.

Impact on Asset Prices

The combination of large budget deficits and significant fiat money creation would be very positive for the stock market—so long as inflation does not meaningfully exceed 4 percent. Government bond purchases by the Fed would keep the price of the bonds high and their yields low. Remember, in the age of paper money, interest rates are determined by the supply of as well as the demand for paper money.

The dollar would continue to lose value against other currencies and particularly against gold and silver, which would continue soaring upward. Other commodity prices would also spike higher. Much higher food prices would cause increased distress for the poorest third of the world's population, possibly generating more hunger-inspired revolutions, possibly with

EXHIBIT 7.4 Scenario Three: The Most Likely One

	2013	2014
GDP at the beginning of the year ($ billions)	15,700	16,014
Real GDP growth target (%)	2%	2%
Inflation rate (%)	4%	4%
Nominal GDP growth target (%)	6%	6%
Nominal GDP growth target ($ billions)	942	961
Ratio of GDP growth to credit growth (%)	50%	50%
Nominal credit growth required ($ billions)	1,884	1,922
Increase in government debt, i.e., the budget deficit ($ billions)	1,884	1,922
Money creation, the Fed monitized half the deficit ($ billions)	942	961
Fed's balance sheet at the beginning of the year ($ billions)	3,900	4,842
Fed's balance sheet year end ($ billions)	4,842	5,803
TCMD at the beginning of the year ($ billions)	54,240	56,124
TCMD at the end of the year ($ billions)	56,124	58,046
Increase in TCMD (%)	3.5%	3.4%
Increase in TCMD adjusted for inflation %	–0.5%	–0.6%
Real GDP year end ($ billions)	16,014	16,334
Budget deficit to GDP (%)	11.8%	11.8%
Government debt at the beginning of the year ($ billions)	11,153	13,037
Government debt at the end of the year ($ billions)	13,037	14,959
Government debt at the end of the year (% of GDP)	81%	92%

significant geo-political ramifications. Core inflation (e.g., food and energy) would rise. However, given the collapse in marginal wage rates brought on by globalization and by immense global excess capacity of all industrial goods, it might not climb above 5 percent by the end of 2014. So long as it doesn't, scenario three would carry us— or, at least the two-thirds of the global population earning more than $4 a day—into 2015.

Conclusion

Scenario three—or something close to it—is the most probable way for events to unfold during 2013 and 2014. The government has the financial capacity to expand its level of debt significantly in order to stave off economic collapse, just as Japan has done for the last 21 years. This scenario is by no means guaranteed, however. Politics might make any additional increase in government spending impossible.

The path described in Scenario three would certainly be the least painful way to reach 2015. Reaching 2015 in that way would not mean the issues at the core of the crisis had been resolved, however. Global supply would still greatly exceed global demand. The United States would continue to deindustrialize and that, in turn, would continue to depress wages and so prevent any new expansion of private sector credit growth. Moreover, the U.S. government would be more indebted and less creditworthy than it is now, and inflation would be on the rise.

Large-scale deficit spending financed in large part by fiat money creation would be a fix, not a solution. The longer-term outlook would remain alarming. A permanent solution to this economic crisis will require something more than fiscal and monetary stimulus alone. A new approach is necessary. Chapter 9 describes the kind of policy that would work. But first, Chapter 8 describes how high the cost could be if a permanent solution is not found in time.

Notes

1. Alan Greenspan, *The Age of Turbulence: Adventures in a New World* (New York: Penguin Press, 2007), p. 340.
2. Wesley Clair Mitchell, *Business Cycles: The Problem and Its Setting*, published by the National Bureau of Economic Research, 1927, p. 1.
3. Ibid., p. 42.
4. Ludwig von Mises, *Human Action* (New Haven, CT: Yale University Press, 1949), p. 554.
5. In his book, *Business Cycles*, published in 1939, Austrian economist Joseph Schumpeter attributed the economic cycles to waves of innovation.
6. von Mises, pp. 563 and 562.
7. Remarks by Governor Ben S. Bernanke, Before the National Economists Club, Washington, DC, November 21, 2011, "Deflation: Making Sure 'It' Doesn't Happen Here."

CHAPTER 8

Disaster Scenarios

Hitler is the foster-child of inflation.

—Lionel Robbins[1]

The New Depression and the Great Depression were both caused by credit-fueled economic booms. In both instances, the boom began when the link between money and gold was broken. The earlier episode began in 1914 when World War I destroyed the Gold Standard in Europe. This time the credit boom began when the United States severed the link between dollars and gold in 1968 and then destroyed the Bretton Woods international monetary system in 1971.

The 1914–1930 boom ended in worldwide economic collapse when the credit that had fueled it could not be repaid. This chapter will consider the consequences for the world should the 1971–2008 boom end the same way.

The Last Great Depression

Consider first what happened last time. In 1930, the United States' money supply comprised currency held by the public (9 percent) and deposits held at commercial banks (91 percent). Banks fund their loans with their customers' deposits. When the credit that fueled the Roaring Twenties could not be repaid, the banks began to fail. When a borrower defaults, it not only destroys credit, it also destroys the deposits that funded the credit. Between 1930 and 1933, 9,000 U.S. banks failed. The corresponding destruction of deposits caused the country's money supply to contract by a third, from $46 billion in 1928 to $31 billion in 1933, as illustrated in Exhibit 8.1. As the money supply shrank, the happy economic dynamic

EXHIBIT 8.1 Money Supply During the Great Depression

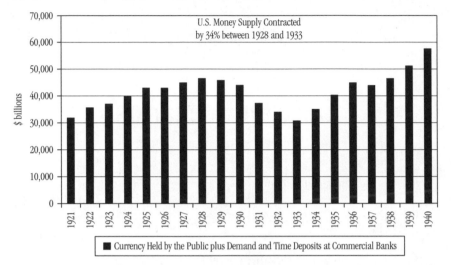

Source: Adapted from *A Monetary History of The United States, 1867–1960* by Milton Friedman and Anna Jacobson Schwartz

that expanding credit had made possible went into reverse, and the global economy spiraled into catastrophe.

Between 1929 and 1933, industrial production in the United States fell by more than half. Commodity prices fell by 38 percent (and by 64 percent from their peak earlier in the decade). U.S. exports and imports both fell by 70 percent. And, the stock market lost nearly 90 percent of its value. (See Exhibit 8.2.)

As shown in Exhibit 8.3, the unemployment rate rose from 3.2 percent in 1929 to 25.2 percent in 1933 and afterward only once fell below 15 percent before 1940, by which time the military buildup for World War II had begun. During the decade of the 1930s, the unemployment rate averaged 18.4 percent. Over the course of the decade, millions of Americans lost their homes.

By 1933, economic output in the U.S. had plunged 46 percent from its 1929 peak. GDP did not return to the 1929 level until 1941, when a nine-fold increase in government spending brought the Great Depression to a close. (See Exhibit 8.4.)

World War II had revolutionary consequences for the U.S. economy. Exhibit 8.5 illustrates just how greatly the role of the government expanded during the war.

President Herbert Hoover increased government spending by 6 percent in 1930, by 8 percent in 1931, and by 30 percent in 1932, the year he ran for reelection. President Franklin Roosevelt launched the New Deal after he

EXHIBIT 8.2 International Trade During the Great Depression

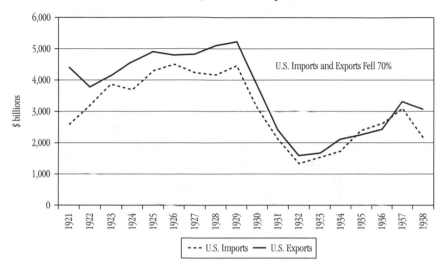

Source: United Nations Statistics Division, Trade Statistics Branch

EXHIBIT 8.3 Unemployment Rate During the Great Depression

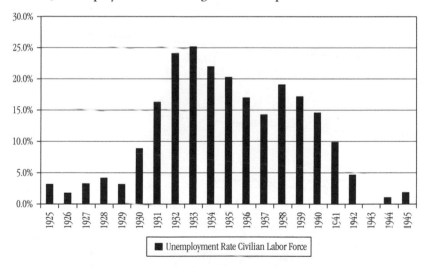

Source: Historical Statistics of the United States, Colonial Times to 1970

was inaugurated in March 1933. In 1934, government spending increased by a further 42 percent, and that year the economy began to recover. The budget was cut by 2 percent in 1935, but expanded again by 28 percent in 1936 ahead of that year's presidential elections. During 1937 and 1938, the budget was again cut by 8 percent and 10 percent, respectively. As a result,

EXHIBIT 8.4 U.S. Gross Domestic Product During Depression and War

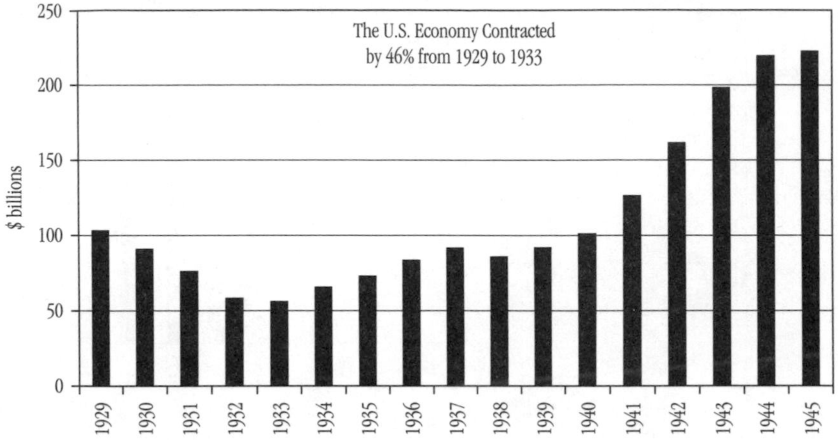

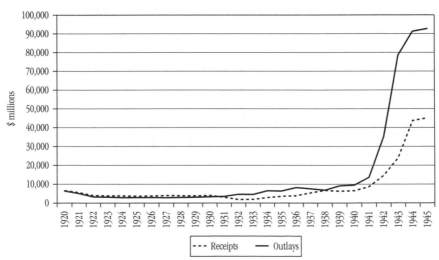

The U.S. Economy Contracted
by 46% from 1929 to 1933

Source: Bureau of Economic Analysis

EXHIBIT 8.5 Federal Government Tax Receipts and Expenditure, 1920 to 1945

Source: Office of Management and Budget

the economy took another sharp turn for the worse with unemployment jumping from 14.3 percent in 1937 to 19.1 percent in 1938.

In 1939, government spending was increased sharply again, by 34 percent. Spending rose by 4 percent in 1940. Then, with Europe at war, the U.S. military buildup began. Government spending rose by 44 percent in

EXHIBIT 8.6 Government Spending During the Great Depression and World War II

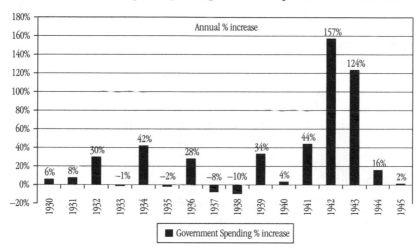

Source: Office of Budget and Management

1941, by 157 percent in 1942, by 124 percent in 1943, and by 16 percent in 1944. (See Exhibit 8.6.)

In 1939, government spending was $6 billion higher than it had been in 1929, an increase of 192 percent over ten years. Between 1940 and 1944, government spending increased by $82 billion, nearly nine times. During those four years, the U.S. economy grew by 117 percent.

The New Deal was hated by the wealthiest classes in America but loved by the great majority of the public. Roosevelt was reelected with 98.5 percent of the electoral votes in 1936. Although the rich considered the aristocratic Roosevelt a traitor to his class, they were lucky to have him in the White House. They would have fared far worse under the gangster socialist policies of Louisiana Governor Huey Long's "Share Our Wealth" program or those of any number of other far-left political aspirants. When credit failed, there was starvation in America, and President Roosevelt took aggressive action to end it. Had he not, communism may have gained a foothold in the United States and permanently transformed the country's political landscape.

Many other countries fared far worse. Hitler was democratically elected as Germany's Fuehrer in 1932. In Spain, General Franco usurped power in a three-year civil war and imposed a right-wing dictatorship on that country that did not end until after Franco's death in 1975. And, in the East, a militarized Japan began its conquest of Asia by taking Manchuria in 1931. The worldwide economic hardship produced by the Great Depression was an important factor—perhaps the determining factor—that led to the Second World War.

And This Time?

What, then, would be the consequences should the world economy spiral now into a New Great Depression? What would happen if a third of total credit market debt (TCMD) in the United States was destroyed by debt defaults, just as a third of the money supply was between 1929 and 1933?

There are many roads that could lead to economic collapse. The following pages sketch the two paths most likely to lead there. Afterward, the consequences that would follow on from such a collapse will be described.

Banking Crisis

The most rapid descent into disaster would occur through a collapse of the banking sector. This could come about in so many ways it is difficult to choose only one beginning for this scenario. It could be set off by tighter regulation of the derivatives market that exposed industrywide fraud and resulted in a general panic. A rogue trader could blow a $20 billion hole in the balance sheet of a medium-sized financial institution, bankrupting it and its numerous counterparties. One of the smaller European countries could default on its sovereign debt, bringing down several large banks in France and Germany that would, in turn, drag down their counterparty banks in London and New York. Or a further decline in home prices in America could lead to a new severe round of losses for U.S. banks that destroyed all their capital. In any of these events, should a new TARP-like bailout not be put in place quickly enough, losses would ricochet around the globe and the financial system as a whole would collapse layer by layer like a house of cards.

In that scenario, TCMD in the United States could easily contract by a third, from $52 trillion to $35 trillion; and, as credit is the new money, this destruction of credit would cause an equivalent contraction of nominal GDP, involving both severe deflation and a plunge in the volume of trade. The equation of exchange of the quantity theory of credit helps visualize that outcome:

$$CV = PT$$

So, a 33 percent contraction in credit (C) would cause a 33 percent contraction in PT, P representing the price level and T the volume of trade. PT is equivalent to the GDP.

Severe deflation would affect all three categories of prices, asset prices, commodity prices, and consumer prices. Unemployment would soar.

Consumption and investment would collapse. Imports into the United States would drop by as much as 75 percent, throwing the entire world into severe depression. The demand for U.S. exports would evaporate. Tax revenues would largely disappear. This would be one path to a New Great Depression.

Protectionism

Alternatively, protectionism could be the catalyst for calamity. This road to ruin would be more winding than a sudden financial-sector Armageddon, but it would end in complete economic breakdown just the same.

In this scenario, renewed economic contraction (it would be called a double-dip recession) would push U.S. unemployment above 12 percent, and a grass-roots movement demanding trade protection for U.S. jobs would take shape. It would be recalled that presidential candidate Ross Perot had warned Americans in 1992 that NAFTA and GATT would result in "a giant sucking sound" as U.S. manufacturing jobs were relocated to low-wage countries. Anger against unfair trade and currency manipulation would infect the Tea Party movement or give rise to separate, similar populist political organizations. Growing panic over the lack of jobs in the United States would bring about a political realignment that swept protectionist politicians into Congress during the 2014 mid-term elections. Aggressive protectionist legislation would be enacted the following year. Trade tariffs would cause an immediate increase in U.S. consumer price inflation as the price of imported goods rose in line with the rate of the tariff. Higher inflation would push up interest rates, further damaging the housing market.

Other countries would match U.S. tariffs with retaliatory tariffs on U.S. exports. To this, the United States would respond with a further round of tariffs. A trade war would begin. Global trade would contract sharply.

Asia's export-driven economies would suffer, and China, the country with the world's largest trade surplus, would be particularly hard hit. Its industrial output could not be absorbed domestically due to the country's low wage structure. The Chinese people do not earn enough to be able to afford to buy what China's factories produce. The resulting glut of Chinese goods would cause a collapse in their product prices, lead to a wave of business failures, and put an end to new investment. Corporate distress would result in a systemic banking crisis. Unemployment would soar. China's economy would quickly collapse into severe depression.

China's imports would contract in line with its exports. The boost that Chinese demand had given to global commodity prices would end. The commodity-producing countries such as Brazil, Australia, Thailand, and Indonesia would be hard hit, as would be countries such as Germany, Japan, and Korea, which had supplied China with higher valued-added products.

International finance could not survive the strain of contracting global trade, plunging commodity prices, falling corporate profits, and the bankruptcies those developments would cause. A systemic banking crisis would be the inevitable outcome.

Here, then, would be a complete replay of the Great Depression: mass joblessness, extensive credit destruction, and a collapse in international trade.

A bout of hyperinflation could be incorporated into either or both of the above scenarios should governments respond to bank failures and economic contraction with successive rounds of massive fiat money creation, as they would be prone to do. Hyperinflation would not prevent economic collapse, however. It would destroy the savings of the middle class, as it did in Weimar Germany during the 1920s. It would also cause devastatingly high rates of interest. Finally, it would completely destroy the value of the dollar and the value of all the other fiat currencies affected by hyperinflation. Although hyperinflation would not be a solution, if the past is any guide, politicians would resort to it as a desperate expedient nevertheless. Andrew White wrote a fascinating account of the politics and economic consequences of hyperinflation during the French Revolution, which he published as a small book in 1912, *Fiat Money Inflation in France*. It is well worth a read and available for free download courtesy of the Project Gutenberg (at www.gutenberg.org/ebooks/6949).

Geopolitical Consequences

The consequences of a New Great Depression would extend far beyond the realm of economics. Hungry people will fight to survive. Governments will use force to maintain internal order at home. This section considers the geopolitical repercussion of economic collapse, beginning with the United States.

First, the U.S. government's tax revenues would collapse with the depression. Second, because global trade would shrivel up, other countries would no longer help finance the U.S. budget deficit by buying government bonds because they would no longer have the money to do so. At present, the rest of the world has a $500 billion annual trade surplus with the United States. The central banks of the United States' trading partners accumulate that surplus as foreign exchange reserves and invest most of those reserves into U.S. government bonds. An economic collapse would cause global trade to plummet and drastically reduce (if not eliminate altogether) the U.S. trade deficit. Therefore, this source of foreign funding for the U.S. budget deficit would dry up.

Consequently, the government would have to sharply curtail its spending, both at home and abroad. Domestically, social programs for the old, the sick, and the unemployed would have to be slashed. Government spending on education and infrastructure would also have to be curtailed. Much less government spending would result in a dramatic increase in poverty and, consequently, in crime. This would combine to produce a crisis of the current two-party political system. Astonishment, frustration, and anger at the economic breakdown would radicalize politics. New parties would form at both extremes of the political spectrum. Given the great and growing income inequality going into the crisis, the hungry have-nots would substantially outnumber the remaining wealthy. On the one hand, a hard swing to the left would be the outcome most likely to result from democratic elections. In that case, the tax rates on the top income brackets could be raised to 80 percent or more, a level last seen in 1963. On the other hand, the possibility of a right-wing putsch could not be ruled out. During the Great Depression, the U.S. military was tiny in comparison with what it became during World War II and during the decades of hot, cold, and terrorist wars that followed. In this New Great Depression, it might be the military that ultimately determines how the country would be governed.

The political battle over America's future would be bitter, and quite possibly bloody. It cannot be guaranteed that the U.S. Constitution would survive.

Foreign affairs would also confront the United States with enormous challenges. During the Great Depression, the United States did not have a global empire. Now it does. The United States maintains hundreds of military bases across dozens of countries around the world. Added to this is a fleet of 11 aircraft carriers and 18 nuclear-armed submarines. The country spends more than $650 billion a year on its military. If the U.S. economy collapses into a New Great Depression, the United States could not afford to maintain its worldwide military presence or to continue in its role as global peacekeeper. Or, at least, it could not finance its military in the same way it does at present.

Therefore, either the United States would have to find an alternative funding method for its global military presence or else it would have to radically scale it back. Historically, empires were financed with plunder and territorial expropriation. The estates of the vanquished ruling classes were given to the conquering generals, while the rest of the population was forced to pay imperial taxes.

The U.S. model of empire has been unique. It has financed its global military presence by issuing government debt, thereby taxing future generations of Americans to pay for this generation's global supremacy. That would no longer be possible if the economy collapsed. Cost–benefit analysis would quickly reveal that much of America's global presence was simply no longer affordable. Many—or even most—of the outposts that did not pay for themselves would have to be abandoned. Priority would be given to those places that were of vital economic interests to the United States. The Middle East oil fields would be at the top of that list. The United States would have to maintain control over them whatever the price.

In this global depression scenario, the price of oil could collapse to $3 per barrel. Oil consumption would fall by half and there would be no speculators left to manipulate prices higher. Oil at that level would impoverish the oil-producing nations, with extremely destabilizing political consequences. Maintaining control over the Middle East oil fields would become much more difficult for the United States. It would require a much larger military presence than it does now. On the one hand, it might become necessary for the United States to reinstate the draft (which would possibly meet with violent resistance from draftees, as it did during the Vietnam War). On the other hand, America's all-volunteer army might find it had more than enough volunteers with the national unemployment rate in excess of 20 percent. The army might have to be employed to keep order at home, given that mass unemployment would inevitably lead to a sharp spike in crime.

Only after the Middle East oil was secured would the country know how much more of its global military presence it could afford to maintain.

If international trade had broken down, would there be any reason for the United States to keep a military presence in Asia when there was no obvious way to finance that presence? In a global depression, the United States' allies in Asia would most likely be unwilling or unable to finance America's military bases there or to pay for the upkeep of the U.S. Pacific fleet. Nor would the United States have the strength to force them to pay for U.S. protection. Retreat from Asia might become unavoidable.

And Europe? What would a cost–benefit analysis conclude about the wisdom of the United States maintaining military bases there? What valued added does Europe provide to the United States? Necessity may mean Europe will have to defend itself.

Should a New Great Depression put an end to the Pax Americana, the world would become a much more dangerous place. When the Great Depression began, Japan was the rising industrial power in Asia. It invaded Manchuria in 1931 and conquered much of the rest of Asia in the early 1940s. Would China, Asia's new rising power, behave the same way in the event of a new global economic collapse? Possibly. China is the only nuclear power in Asia east of India (other than North Korea, which is largely a Chinese satellite state).

However, in this disaster scenario, it is not certain that China would survive in its current configuration. Its economy would be in ruins. Most of its factories and banks would be closed. Unemployment could exceed 30 percent. There would most likely be starvation both in the cities and in the countryside. The Communist Party could lose its grip on power, in which case the country could break apart, as it has numerous times in the past. It was less than 100 years ago that China's provinces, ruled by warlords, were at war with one another.

United or divided, China's nuclear arsenal would make it Asia's undisputed superpower if the United States were to withdraw from the region. From Korea and Japan in the North to New Zealand in the South to Burma in the West, all of Asia would be at China's mercy. And hunger among China's population of 1.3 billion people could necessitate territorial expansion into Southeast Asia. In fact, the central government might not be able to prevent mass migration southward, even if it wanted to.

In Europe, severe economic hardship would revive the centuries-old struggle between the left and the right. During the 1930s, the Fascists movement arose and imposed a police state on most of Western Europe. In the East, the Soviet Union had become a communist police state even earlier. The far right and the far left of the political spectrum converge in totalitarianism. It is difficult to judge whether Europe's democratic institutions would hold up better this time that they did last time.

England had an empire during the Great Depression. Now it only has banks. In a severe worldwide depression, the country—or, at least London—could become ungovernable. Frustration over poverty and a lack of jobs would erupt into anti-immigration riots not only in the United Kingdom but also across most of Europe.

The extent to which Russia would menace its European neighbors is unclear. On the one hand, Russia would be impoverished by the collapse in oil prices and might be too preoccupied with internal unrest to threaten anyone. On the other hand, it could provoke a war with the goal of maintaining internal order through emergency wartime powers.

Germany is very nearly demilitarized today when compared with the late 1930s. Lacking a nuclear deterrent of its own, it could be subject to Russian intimidation. While Germany could appeal for protection from England and France, who do have nuclear capabilities, it is uncertain that would buy Germany enough time to remilitarize before it became a victim of Eastern aggression.

As for the rest of the world, its prospects in this disaster scenario can be summed up in only a couple of sentences. Global economic output could fall by as much as half, from $60 trillion to $30 trillion. Not all of the world's seven billion people would survive in a $30 trillion global economy. Starvation would be widespread. Food riots would provoke political upheaval and myriad big and small conflicts around the world. It would be a humanitarian catastrophe so extreme as to be unimaginable for the current generation, who, at least in the industrialized world, has known only prosperity. Nor would there be reason to hope that the New Great Depression would end quickly. The Great Depression was only ended by an even more calamitous global war that killed approximately 60 million people.

Conclusion

This chapter will be called alarmist. It is intended to be. These disaster scenarios are not predictions. However, they are meant to serve as a warning of how bad things could become if policy fails to prevent the New Depression from becoming the New Great Depression. Calamity on the scale described in this chapter is not just conceivable, it has recurred throughout history. All the civilization of the past eventually collapsed due to mismanagement or war. It would be a mistake to believe ours is invulnerable to a similar fate. This crisis should not be underestimated.

Note

1. A quotation from the foreword to *The Economics of Inflation—A Study of Currency Depreciation in Post-War Germany* by Costantino Bresciani-Turroni. First published by Universita Bocconi in 1931. Robbins' quote appeared in the first English edition published by John Dickens & Co Ltd in 1937.

CHAPTER 9

The Policy Options

The imperatives of technology and organization, not the images of ideology, are what determine the shape of economic society.
—John Kenneth Galbraith[1]

Capitalism was an economic system in which the private sector drove the economic process through saving, capital accumulation, and investment. The government's role was very limited. The United States has not had that kind of economic system for decades. Today, the federal government spends $25 out of every $100 spent in the economy, and state and local government spend $11 more. The central bank creates the money and manipulates its value. Almost all the major industries are subsidized in one way or another by the government and almost half of all households receive some kind of government assistance. Finally, the economic process itself is no longer driven by saving and investment. Instead, it is driven by borrowing and consumption.

This is not capitalism. Market forces no longer drive the economy. The current system is government-directed, but not planned. Government policy is determined through a process of compromise between the demands of competing power blocks: big business, the banking industry, the military, the elderly, and the general public, which, until recently, had grown to expect an ever-improving standard of living. Deficit spending and fiat money allowed the government to satisfy all those competing demands for more than a generation. During that time, a key component of government policy has been to channel ever-greater quantities of credit to the household sector. As total credit expanded 50 times in less than 50 years, it created wealth and kept the American Dream alive. That extraordinary expansion of credit changed the nature of the economic system itself, however. Capitalism became Creditism, for lack of a better word. This new credit-based economic system is now in crisis because the household sector cannot bear any additional debt. The gap between its income and its debt has become too great.

The first step toward finding a lasting solution to this crisis is to form a realistic understanding of the nature of this economic system—not as it used to be and not as any particular group thinks it should be, but as it really is. Only then will it be possible to devise a strategy that could correct its faults.

The first section of this chapter presents a brief history of how capitalism evolved into the credit-based, government-directed economic system that is in place today. Once that is understood, the policy options available within this system become clearer. The rest of the chapter outlines a strategy that could avert economic breakdown by making use of the new policy tools our current economic system makes possible.

Capitalism and the Laissez-Faire Method

Laissez-faire capitalism did not survive World War I. In Europe, the belligerent nations suspended the convertibility of their currencies into gold in order to finance the war with government debt and fiat money creation. The classical gold standard was thus one of the first victims of the war.

The United States did not leave the gold standard at that time, but the U.S. economy was destabilized by Europe's abandonment of the gold standard nevertheless. From 1914, when the war began, to 1917, when the United States entered the war, Europe sent a great deal of its gold to the United States to pay for war materials, something it could not have afforded to do had it remained on the gold standard. During that period, the stock of monetary gold in the United States rose by 64 percent. That sharp expansion of "high powered money" played an important role in creating the boom of the Roaring Twenties by making rapid credit growth possible.

After 1917, U.S. government spending skyrocketed. Government outlays rose from $713 million in 1916 to $12,677 million in 1918 and to $18,493 million in 1919. (See Exhibit 9.1.) That spending was financed by a combination of taxes, borrowing, and direct money creation by the newly established central bank. The marginal tax rate on the highest income bracket rose from 7 percent in 1916 to 77 percent in 1918, while the marginal tax rate on the lowest income group increased from 1 percent to 6 percent.

Industrial production rose sharply during the war. Even more important, however, was the fact that the war profoundly changed the organizational structure of the economy. The War Industries Board, under the chairmanship of Bernard Baruch, was set up to coordinate production for the war. Its powers included resource allocation, centralized purchasing, and price fixing. "More than any other single period, World War I was the critical

EXHIBIT 9.1 Government Outlays: 1901 to 1929

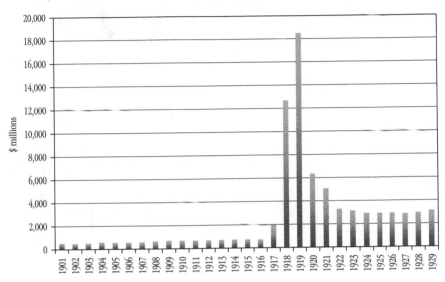

Source: Office of Management and Budget

watershed for the American business system," Murray Rothbard wrote in 1972. "It was a 'war collectivism,' a totally planned economy run largely by big-business interest through the instrumentality of the central government, which served as the model, the precedent, and the inspiration for state corporate capitalism for the remainder of the twentieth century."[2]

The government debt and the fiat money created during the war resulted in the tremendous economic boom of the 1920s. The Roaring Twenties ended in the Great Depression when the credit that had fueled the boom could not be repaid. The banking system failed and international trade collapsed. Karl Marx's prophecies of capitalism's ultimate collapse appeared to be coming true. When Franklin Roosevelt became president in 1933, he took the United States off the gold standard and introduced an array of New Deal relief programs that held the country together until World War II set off a new, debt-driven, government-directed economic boom, this one on an even larger scale than the one generated by the First World War.

Government spending jumped from $9,468 in 1940 to $35,137 in 1942 to more than $90,000 in both 1944 and 1945. (See Exhibit 9.2.) And, as during the First World War, the government once again took complete control over the economy; this time through the War Production Board. The budget deficit peaked at 30 percent of GDP in 1943. Altogether, government debt rose 413 percent between 1940 and 1945.

There was widespread fear that the U.S. economy would collapse back into depression when the war ended. It didn't, however. At the end

EXHIBIT 9.2 Government Outlays: 1920 to 1949

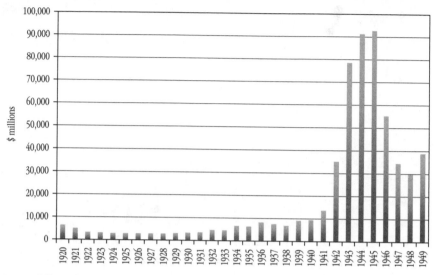

Source: Office of Management and Budget

of the war, the government set up the Bretton Woods international monetary system to promote international trade. It also allocated $13 billion (5 percent of U.S. GDP) in Marshall Plan assistance to rebuild Europe. Those measures created opportunities for American businesses to expand abroad. Meanwhile, at home, the government encouraged families to buy houses on credit. As a result, the level of household-sector debt relative to GDP tripled from 16 percent in 1946 to 46 percent 20 years later. Consequently, although the ratio of government debt to GDP fell very sharply during the decades following the war, TCMD to GDP only contracted slightly, from 158 percent in 1946 to a low of 132 percent in 1951. (See Exhibit 9.3.)

After the war, government spending (in absolute terms) declined until 1948. Then it began to surge once again. Exhibit 9.4 illustrates rather dramatically the explosion of government spending over the following decades. On this chart, the spending during the war only looks like a small blip relative to what came later.

By 1951, government outlays had returned to the extraordinary levels reached at the peak of the world war. During the 1950s, the government spent billions on the Korean War, the Cold War, and the interstate highway system. During the 1960s, the government spent billions on the Great Society social welfare programs at home, the Vietnam War abroad, and on NASA to explore space.

The excessive government spending of the 1960s caused the Bretton Woods system to collapse in 1971, just as World War I had knocked

EXHIBIT 9.3 Debt to GDP: World War II to 2010

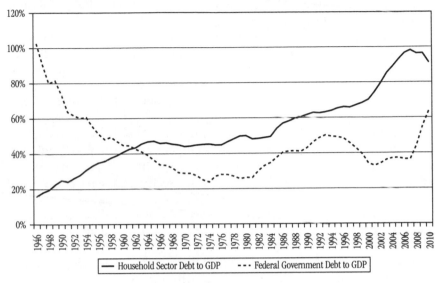

Source: Federal Reserve, *Flow of Funds Accounts of the United States, second quarter 2011*

EXHIBIT 9.4 Government Outlays: 1940 to 2010

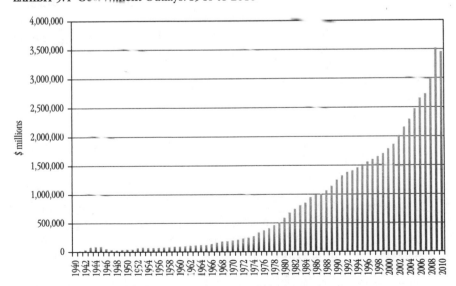

Source: Office of Budget and Management

Europe off the gold standard in 1914. The shift to a fiat money standard, combined with continued deficit spending, caused double-digit inflation in the United States a few years later.

The malaise of the 1970s only ended when President Reagan introduced a new round of military Keynesianism in 1981. The Reagan budget deficits took government debt up 188 percent while he was in office. As a result, the level of TCMD to GDP broke out of its post–World War II range and soared from 169 percent to 233 percent during his presidency.

The next spike in TCMD began in the late 1990s as the government-sponsored enterprises, Fannie Mae and Freddie Mac, pumped credit into the household sector. In 2007, TCMD to GDP hit 360 percent. At that point, neither the GSEs nor the household sector could bear any more debt; and the crisis began.

This lightning-fast review of the past 100 years is not in any way intended to suggest that all these wars and social spending programs were launched in order to create economic growth. Clearly, that was not the case. It is intended, however, to demonstrate that they *did* create economic growth, regardless of how or why they came about. In other words, the economy—and the evolution of the economic system from capitalism to creditism—have been driven by the government without being planned by the government.

It is necessary to understand how great the role of the government has been in the economy and how far removed our economic system is now from laissez-faire capitalism in order to understand the nature of this crisis and the options that are available to resolve it. Cutting government spending and allowing market forces to reestablish a market-determined equilibrium are not among those options. Reallocating government spending away from consumption and toward investment is.

Murray Rothbard (1926 to 1995), a student and friend of Ludwig von Mises and an impressive economist in his own right, believed that the Great Depression would have ended much sooner had the government not interfered and simply allowed the economy to adjust by itself. He described what he thought would have happened in that case in his book, *America's Great Depression*:

> *The laissez-faire method would have permitted the banks of the nation to close—as they probably would have done without governmental intervention. The bankrupt banks could then have been transferred to the ownership of their depositors, who would have taken charge of the invested, frozen assets of the banks. There would have been a vast, but rapid, deflation, with the money supply falling to virtually 100 percent*

of the nation's gold stock. The depositors would have been "forced savers" in the existing bank assets (loans and investments). This cleansing surgical operation would have ended, once and for all, the inherently bankrupt fractional-reserve system, would have henceforth grounded loans and investments on people's voluntary savings rather than artificially-extended credit, and would have brought the country to a truly sound and hard monetary base.[3]

Perhaps he was right. On the other hand, perhaps the suffering that would have resulted from that "vast, but rapid, deflation" and "cleansing surgical operation" would have been so great that American Democracy could not have survived it.

Eighty years and $50 trillion in debt later, the suffering that would result from the laissez-faire method this time would be even more extreme. The nation's gold stock is worth approximately $431 billion (at $1,650 per ounce). The debt deflation that would be necessary to return the credit supply to that level would destroy the world as we know it.

Rothbard and von Mises were brilliant economists and writers. It is not surprising that they have had a powerful influence on the thinking of those, such as Ron Paul and some of his fellow Libertarians, who have read their work. It is crucial to understand, however, that Rothbard and von Mises lived and wrote in a different time. Were they alive today, it is certain that they would still condemn fiat money as a great economic evil. It is not certain, however, that they would recommend the laissez-faire method as the correct solution to the current crisis in the global economy. In fact, it seems inconceivable that they would.

A capitalist economy in the nineteenth century may well have adjusted rapidly (although painfully) to any shock that occurred. Our economic system would not. In fact, the disruption would be so great that our political system could not stand up to it. For instance, how far would wages in the United States have to fall for U.S. factory workers to be competitive with their counterparts in the developing world who earn $5 per day? Similarly, what would be the value of being a shareholder in a bankrupt bank holding frozen assets that had lost 99 percent of their value?

The sooner it is understood that the laissez-faire method is not an option, the sooner the quest for a workable method can begin.

The global economy that has emerged during the last generation is the product of an economic system that is driven by credit. If credit contracts significantly, globalization will not survive. Should globalization collapse, many of the people in the world who are supported by the wealth that globalization produces would not survive.

The State of Government Finances

The next step toward devising a workable method for resolving this crisis is to take stock of the nation's financial condition. Given that the government came close to being unable to pay all of its bills in August 2011 when Congress delayed lifting the *debt ceiling,* it would be easy to conclude that the government's finances are in crisis. They are not. They have deteriorated significantly since the economic crisis began, but the government is still a long way away from defaulting on its debts.

At the end of fiscal year 2011, government debt amounted to 72 percent of GDP, up from 36 percent at the end of 2007. To put that into perspective, when Japan's economic crisis began in 1990, the Japanese government's level of debt to GDP was 68 percent. It has since risen to roughly 230 percent, and it is still rising. The Japanese government has not defaulted, nor has it had to resort to so much fiat money creation as to cause high rates of inflation in Japan. In fact, deflation has been a bigger worry than inflation for the past two decades.

Although the U.S. government's finances are not currently in crisis, eventually they will be if the government does not find a way to bring down the budget deficits it is projected to have in the future. The Congressional Budget Office (CBO) is the best source of information about the budget. It regularly provides detailed updates of its projections for the budget deficit, both the near term deficits and the deficits projected far into the future.

In June 2011, the CBO updated its long-term budget outlook. It provided two scenarios, neither of which, as it was careful to point out, represents CBO projections. The first was based on its *extended-baseline scenario* and the second was based on an *alternative fiscal scenario.* The CBO's description of these scenarios sheds light on not only the direction in which the government's finances are moving but also the timeframe and the complexity of the issues involved. It is useful to consider them in some detail.

The Extended-Baseline Scenario

One long-term budget scenario used in this analysis, the extended-baseline scenario, *adheres closely to current law.*

Under this scenario, the expiration of the tax cuts enacted since 2001 and most recently extended in 2010, the growing reach of the alternative minimum tax, the tax provisions of the recent health care legislation, and the way in which the tax system interacts with economic growth would result in steadily higher revenues relative to GDP. Revenues would reach 23 percent of GDP by 2035—much higher than has typically been seen in recent decades—and would grow to larger percentages thereafter. At the same time, under this scenario, government spending on everything other than the major mandatory health care programs, Social Security, and interest on federal debt—activities such as national defense and a wide variety of domestic programs—would decline to the lowest percentage of GDP since before World War II.

That significant increase in revenues and decrease in the relative magnitude of other spending would offset much—though not all—of the rise in spending on health care programs and Social Security. As a result, debt would increase slowly from its already high levels relative to GDP, as would the required interest payments on that debt. Federal debt held by the public would grow from an estimated 69 percent of GDP this year to 84 percent by 2035. With both debt and interest rates rising over time, interest payments, which absorb federal resources that could otherwise be used to pay for government services, would climb to 4 percent of GDP (or one-sixth of federal revenues) by 2035, compared with about 1 percent now.[4]

The Alternative Fiscal Scenario

The budget outlook is much bleaker under the alternative fiscal scenario, which incorporates several changes to current law that are widely expected to occur or that would modify some provisions of law that might be difficult to sustain for a long period. Most important are the assumptions about revenues: that the tax cuts enacted since 2001 and extended most recently in 2010 will be extended; that the reach of the alternative minimum tax will be restrained to stay close to its historical extent; and that over the longer run, tax law will evolve further so that revenues remain near their historical average of 18 percent of GDP. This scenario also incorporates assumptions that Medicare's payment rates for physicians will remain at current levels (rather than declining by about a third, as under current law), and that some policies enacted in the March 2010 health care legislation to restrain growth in federal health care spending will not continue in effect after 2021. In addition, the alternative scenario includes an assumption that spending on activities other than the major mandatory health care programs, Social Security, and interest on the debt will not fall quite as low as under the extended-baseline scenario, although it will still fall to its lowest level (relative to GDP) since before World War II.

Under those policies, federal debt would grow much more rapidly than under the extended-baseline scenario. With significantly lower revenues and higher outlays, debt held by the public would exceed 100 percent of GDP by 2021. After that, the growing imbalance between revenues and spending, combined with spiraling interest payments, would swiftly push debt to higher and higher levels. Debt as a share of GDP would exceed its historical peak of 109 percent by 2023 and would approach 190 percent in 2035.

Many budget analysts believe that the alternative fiscal scenario presents a more realistic picture of the nation's underlying fiscal policies than the extended-baseline scenario does. The explosive path of federal debt under the alternative fiscal scenario underscores the need for large and rapid policy changes to put the nation on a sustainable fiscal course.[5]

The report concludes:

To keep deficits and debt from climbing to unsustainable levels, policymakers will need to increase revenues substantially as a percentage of GDP, decrease spending significantly from projected levels, or adopt some combination of those two approaches. Making such changes while economic activity and employment remain well below their potential levels would probably slow the economic recovery. However, the sooner that medium and long-term changes to tax and spending policies are agreed on, and the sooner they are carried out once the economy recovers, the smaller will be the damage to the economy from growing federal debt. Earlier action would permit smaller or more gradual changes and would give people more time to adjust to them, but it would require more sacrifices sooner from current older workers and retirees for the benefit of younger workers and future generations.[6]

No one should question that the government's finances are on an unsustainable course given current projections for spending and revenues. At the same time, there is no reason to fear that the United States will experience a sovereign debt crisis any time soon. Even the COB's more pessimistic "alternative fiscal scenario" would only take U.S. government debt to GDP up to 190 percent by 2035. In other words, the government could carry on with its current irresponsible fiscal policies for another quarter century and still not have reached the level of debt to GDP that Japan is experiencing now. Therefore, while there is good reason for concern—even alarm—over the government's fiscal position, there is enough time to transition it to a sustainable fiscal path . . . if a sustainable fiscal path can be devised.

The Government's Options

This task is complicated by the nature of our debt-fueled economic system. The economy has grown dependent on government spending and debt. Therefore, given the current structure of the economy, if the government spends significantly less, the country will remain marred in an economic depression with no visible end in sight.

It appears, then, that three options are available to the government. The first is *austerity*. The government could sharply reduce its spending. The result would be a New Great Depression. This is the least attractive option.

The second option is for the government to carry on doing what it does now—that is, the *status quo,* borrowing and spending to support consumption. This approach would sustain the economy for at least a decade. Then there would be a U.S. sovereign debt crisis and the world would collapse into a New Great Depression. This option is preferable to option one, but far from ideal.

Option three is for the government to borrow and invest in a way that not only supports the economy but actually restructures it so as to restore its long-term viability. This option, *rational investment,* is the only one of the three with the potential to result in a happy ending. It differs from option two, the status quo, in a very significant way. In option two, the government continues to borrow and spend in a way that boosts consumption in the economy. Spending in that way creates economic growth, but only once. When the money is spent, it is gone. It yields no long-term return.

In option three the government would borrow and invest; and the government's investments would yield a return. In fact, given the magnitude of the resources the government has available to invest, the returns that could be generated would be sufficient to restore the government's finances to health—perhaps even making it possible for the government to repay all of its debt within a relatively short period of time.

The government could continue spending money on the same things it does now, but on an ever-greater scales as it has for decades; and that would continue to generate economic growth up until the time when its sovereign debt crisis begins. There is literally no limit as to how much the government could spend through Medicare to improve the health of the nation; and there seems to be no limit on the amount that can be spent on national defense.

Alternatively, the government could cap its spending on current programs and spend more, instead, on investment programs that could be made to quickly pay for themselves.

Consider just one example of the possibilities open to us, a government financed and directed program to develop solar energy. Here is how it could work.

American Solar

Just as President John Kennedy, in May 1961 announced that the United States would put a man on the moon by the end of that decade, our president should announce that the U.S. economy will be entirely fueled by domestically generated solar energy by 2025. Through this government-directed program, a new generation of cost-effective solar panels would be built and installed on government-owned land in the Nevada desert; a new nationwide grid would be built to transmit the direct current; the automobile industry would be restructured to produce only electric-powered vehicles; and electric refueling stations would be built to replace gas stations coast to coast. The program would be like NASA or the Tennessee Valley Authority—but on a much bigger scale.

Just the announcement of this American Solar initiative would produce immediate benefits. First, fears that the world is running out of oil—an idea that has been around since at least 1870—would give way to the realization that oil would be obsolete and practically worthless by 2030. As a result, it is likely that the price of oil would fall by 75 percent or more the very day the new energy program is announced.

That initial collapse in oil prices by itself would have an immediate and significant positive impact on the economy. Gasoline prices would fall from $4 to $1 per gallon. That would create an opportunity for the government to finance its solar program by imposing a tax of $1 per gallon, thereby raising more than $100 billion a year, even while the cost of gasoline to the public still fell by half or more.

Next, additional funding could be raised from the private sector, which would be invited to take a minority stake in the United States' solar initiative. The majority interest and the direction of the project would remain in government control, however. Given the weakness in the general economy and the certainty of the program's success, a great deal of private investment would be forthcoming. Even the cash-rich oil companies would probably participate, recognizing the imperative to diversify out of oil in order to survive.

The returns to private sector investors would be capped at a small margin above their cost of capital, however, in light of the near-zero risk involved and in order to retain the highest possible returns for the government's shareholders (i.e., the American public).

The goal would be not only to develop a cheap, limitless energy source for the future but also to stimulate the economy now. So, for instance, the government could initiate this program by making a $300 billion investment divided between funding for basic research, building and installing the first generation of solar panels, building the nationwide electricity grid, and developing electric cars.

The investment into basic research would be divided between the country's universities, and it would give an immediate boost to the economy by putting scientists and technicians to work. Building $100 billion worth of solar panels would not only give a shot in the arm to the manufacturing sector but also generate technological advances and economies of scale that would lower future costs. The installation of those panels and the construction of the grid would create tens of thousands of jobs from coast to coast.

At the end of three years, stock would be taken to determine what was working, what was not, and how best to proceed with the second phase of the project involving a second $300 billion investment. Research and development (R&D) breakthroughs would be incorporated in a second generation of solar panel production. The grid build-out would continue. The conversion of the automobile industry would continue and construction of the electric refueling stations could begin. And so on.

These three-year, $300 billion stages would be repeated as long as necessary to accomplish the goal. Most probably, within ten years and at a cost of around $1 trillion, the United States would have limitless, cheap, and nonpolluting energy. Should a $1 trillion investment over 10 years not succeed in achieving this goal, then $2 trillion over 15 years certainly would.

The benefits would be both immediate and never-ending. From the beginning, government borrowing and spending, if on a large enough scale, would create jobs and prevent the economy from collapsing into a New Great Depression. Moreover, as mentioned before, the program itself would cause the price of oil to plummet, which would not only boost domestic consumption in other products, since the public would spend less on oil, but also sharply reduce the country's trade deficit. Within five years, American Solar would be the world's low-cost producer of solar equipment. Demand from abroad would increase the project's economies of scale, while exports would further improve the country's balance of trade.

Upon the project's completion, the cost of energy in the United States would be 90 percent less than at present. Moreover, the United States would be energy independent. The country's trade deficit would improve by 40 percent when it stopped importing oil. The country would no longer have to spend money defending the foreign sources of its oil supply. As a result, its military spending and budget deficit could be cut by $150 billion a year. Finally, the government could tax the domestically generated electricity and so, not only fully recoup the cost of the investment—that would be recovered within only a decade or two—but generate windfall tax revenues for generations.

Solar energy would rank among humanity's greatest accomplishments. Low-cost energy would make possible a host of other private sector innovations, with wealth-creating possibilities beyond comprehension.

This is just one example of the opportunities that our new credit-based economic system makes possible. There are many others. A large government-directed investment program to develop genetic and biotechnology would create medical miracles. Heavy government investment into nanotechnology would generate a new Industrial Revolution.

Conclusion

We have built an economy out of $50 trillion of credit over the past 50 years. When credit expands, it creates both an asset and a liability. The sustainability of the entire economic superstructure depends on how that credit is used going forward. If it is used for consumption, then it can generate no return and the superstructure will collapse. That is the mistake that led to this New Depression. If it is invested in projects that generate a high enough return to pay the interest on the debt, then it will not only support the economic structure now in place, it will support a larger and more prosperous economy.

Our society has failed to understand that our economic system has changed. Therefore, it has not yet grasped the possibilities inherent within this new system. Credit can now be deployed by the government on a scale so vast that it can revolutionize the production potential of this planet.

The U.S. government can now borrow money for ten years at a cost of 2 percent interest a year. If it borrows at that rate and invests in projects that yield even 3 percent, Creditopia will survive. If it borrows at that rate and invests on a grand scale in grand projects, precarious Creditopia could be transformed into a sustainable Utopia in which the cost of energy falls 90 percent and life expectancy doubles.

There is no doubt that the abandonment of commodity money (gold) created distortions that interfered with the self-regulating market economy. The point to grasp, however, is that our global civilization has been built on and around those distortions and that it could very possibly collapse into ruin if those distortions are not perpetuated through further credit expansion.

That requires the government to borrow and invest.

Would that be capitalism? No. We do not have capitalism now, however. Our economic system is not one in which the accumulation and investment of capital drives the production process. It is one in which the creation and expenditure of credit does.

The question is not whether we are going to abandon capitalism and replace it with a different kind of economic system. We did that long ago. The question is: Are we going to allow the economic system now in place to collapse?

Thus, this economic crisis marks a crossroad for our civilization. Our options are to grasp and fearlessly exploit the immense possibilities inherent in our new credit-based economic system or else fail to grasp them and collapse into what could prove to be decades of misery.

Notes

1. John Kenneth Galbraith, *The New Industrial State* (Princeton, NJ: Princeton University Press, 1967), p. 8.
2. Ronald Radosh and Murray N. Rothbard, eds. (New York: *A New History of Leviathan*, New York: E.P. Dutton & Co., 1972).
3. Murray Rothbard, *America's Great Depression* (Auburn, AL: Ludwig von Mises Institute, 1963).
4. Congressional Budget Office, "2011 Long-Term Budget Outlook," June 2011, www.cbo.gov/ftpdocs/122xx/doc12212/06-21-Long-Term_Budget_Outlook.pdf.
5. Ibid.
6. Ibid.

CHAPTER 10

Fire and Ice, Inflation and Deflation

Any continued rise in prices is dangerous because, once we begin to rely on its stimulating effect, we shall be committed to a course that will leave us no choice but that between more inflation, on the one hand, and paying for our mistake by a recession or depression, on the other.

—Friedrich A. Hayek[1]

The U.S. economy has been built on $52 trillion of credit that the private sector is now incapable of repaying. Without government intervention, the economy will collapse in a deflationary spiral as market forces bring supply back into equilibrium with demand at a much lower level of economic output and employment. Mismanaged intervention could have the opposite effect, however, and produce very high and destabilizing rates of inflation.

Extreme inflation is like fire in that it consumes the savings of the public in a conflagration of rising prices. Extreme deflation is ice-like. It leaves the economy frozen in a liquidity trap with high unemployment and no growth. Both would end in disaster for the economy and, therefore, for society. However, the two would impact asset prices very differently. This chapter looks at how very high rates of inflation and extreme deflation would affect the various asset classes. It is not inconceivable that, as this economic calamity plays out over the next decade, the economy could be hit by both. Government policy will determine the outcome. As of now, it remains very uncertain which direction government policy will take.

Fire

The United States has experienced five episodes of very high rates of inflation. Each one has resulted from the issue of fiat money. During the first four periods, the fiat money that caused the inflation was created to finance a major war: The Revolutionary War, the War of 1812, the Civil War, and World War I. When those wars ended, government spending was curtailed, sound money was restored, and the inflation abated.

The double-digit inflation of the 1970s was different. It followed the heavy government deficit spending of the 1960s, which had forced the abandonment of gold backing for the dollar in 1968 and resulted in the breakdown of the Bretton Woods system in 1971. Fed Chairman Paul Volcker crushed that round of inflation with very high interest rates in 1981.

A sixth round of high inflation should have occurred a few years later as the result of President Ronald Reagan's deficit-funded spending spree. That did not happen, however, because the United States began incurring very large trade deficits with other countries. In all the previous inflationary periods, excessive government spending had created domestic bottlenecks in industrial production and labor shortages; and those factors combined to generate wage-push inflation. During the 1980s, the country avoided domestic bottlenecks and labor shortages (and, therefore, inflation) by buying more from abroad.

Whereas during most of the twentieth century, U.S. trade had either been in balance or in surplus, during the 1980s the country developed a large trade deficit. That deficit reached what was at that time an unprecedented peacetime record of 3.7 percent of GDP in 1987.

Thus, whether by accident or design, a completely new model for economic growth came into existence. The government discovered that it could stimulate the economy with large budget deficits without causing high rates of inflation, so long as the country imported enough from abroad to circumvent the normal bottlenecks.

Over the following decades, the expansion of trade—and trade deficits—with low-wage countries such as China created strong disinflationary pressures in the United States, despite the extraordinary expansion of fiat money-denominated credit that was occurring there at that time. Rising debt drove the U.S. economy and created employment by pushing up asset prices, but consumer price inflation remained low as an increasing share of the goods sold in the country was made with $5 per day labor. The U.S. trade deficit reached 6 percent of GDP in 2006.

The Fed likes to take credit for the "Great Moderation" in inflation during recent decades. But monetary policy had very little to do with it. The disinflation was the result of a collapse in the marginal cost of labor.

Thus, it was an unprecedented combination of events—fiat money, technological advances in transportation and communications, large global trade imbalances, and cross-border capital flows—that permitted the truly extraordinary expansion of credit that has occurred in the Unites States since the early 1980s. If high rates of inflation had occurred, the credit expansion would have had to be curtailed through much higher interest rates. Then the global credit bubble could not have formed.

Ice

Turning to deflation, there have been only three episodes of severe deflation in the country's history: during the late 1830s, from 1873 to 1896, and during the Great Depression. The first round followed a period of rapid credit expansion that came to an abrupt end when President Andrew Jackson refused to renew the charter of the country's central bank, the Second Bank of the United States, in 1836.

The long deflation of the last quarter of the nineteenth century was a worldwide phenomenon and was driven by the sharp fall in agricultural prices that resulted from the great advances in transportation technology. The spread of railroads allowed agricultural products from the American Midwest and other previously difficult-to-reach territories to be transported to heavily populated urban centers. Food prices fell sharply as a result, and falling food prices put downward pressure on the overall price level. The end of the American Civil War and the demonetization of silver in 1873 also contributed significantly to the deflationary pressures of that period.

The severe deflation that took place during the Great Depression occurred when the debt that fueled the Roaring Twenties could not be repaid. As discussed previously, the government debt and fiat money creation that financed the First World War generated the credit boom of the 1920s. From 1930, bankruptcies and defaults destroyed much of the financial superstructure and left the economy in ruins.

Observing that phenomenon firsthand, Irving Fisher explained it in a famous 21-page article published in *Econometrica* in October 1933. The article was titled "The Debt-Deflation Theory of Great Depressions."

The crisis the world faces today is very much like the one that crushed the global economy in 1930. Both were caused by extraordinarily large fiat-money-denominated credit bubbles. Fisher's article clearly describes the debt-deflation dynamics that now threaten to drive the global economy into a New Great Depression. This important article will therefore be considered at some length because there is no clearer explanation of the manner in which our economy would collapse should government intervention cease.

Fisher's Theory of Debt-Deflation

Fisher believed that overindebtedness and deflation were the two dominant factors in the great booms and depressions. He wrote

> *as explanations of the so-called business cycle, . . . I doubt the adequacy of over-production, under-consumption, over-capacity, price-dislocation, maladjustment between agricultural and industrial prices, over-confidence, over-investment, over-saving, over-spending, and the discrepancy between saving and investment.*
>
> *I venture the opinion, . . . that, in the great booms and depressions, each of the above-named factors has played a subordinate role as compared with two dominate factors, namely over-indebtedness to start with and deflation following soon after; also that where any of the other factors do become conspicuous, they are often merely effects or symptoms of these two. In short, the big bad actors are debt disturbances and price-level disturbances.*

He then described the dynamics of the post-boom deflationary spiral:

> *Assuming, accordingly, that, at some point of time, a state of over-indebtedness exists, this will tend to lead to liquidation, through the alarm either of debtors or creditors or both. Then we may deduce the following chain of consequences in nine links: (1)* Debt liquidation *leads to distress selling and to (2)* Contraction of deposit currency, *as bank loans are paid off, and to a slowing down of velocity of circulation. This contraction of deposits and of their velocity, precipitated by distress selling, causes (3)* A fall in the level of prices, *in other words, a swelling of the dollar. Assuming, as above stated, that this fall of prices is not interfered with by reflation or otherwise, there must be (4)* A still greater fall in the net worths of business, *precipitating bankruptcies and (5)* A like fall in profits, *which in a "capitalistic," that is, a private-profit society, leads the concerns which are running at a loss to make (6)* A reduction in output, in trade and in employment of labor. *These losses, bankruptcies and unemployment, lead to (7)* Pessimism and loss of confidence, *which in turn lead to (8)* Hoarding and slowing down *still more the velocity of circulation.*
>
> *The above eight changes cause (9)* Complicated disturbances in the rates of interest, *in particular, a fall in the nominal, or money, rates and a rise in the real, or commodity, rates of interest.*
>
> *Evidently debt and deflation go far toward explaining a great mass of phenomena in a very simple logical way.*

Fisher also provided a chronology of how the deflation unfolds:

The following table of our nine factors, occurring and recurring (together with distress selling), gives a fairly typical, though still inadequate, picture of the cross-currents of a depression in the approximate order in which it is believed they usually occur.

    I. *Mild Gloom and Shock to Confidence*
       Slightly Reduced Velocity of Circulation
       Debt Liquidation
    II. *Money Interest on Safe Loans Falls*
       But Money Interest on Unsafe Loans Rises
    III. *Distress Selling*
       More Gloom
       Fall in Security Prices
       More Liquidation
       Fall in Commodity Prices
    IV. *Real Interest Rises; Real Debts Increase*
       More Pessimism and Distrust
       More Liquidation
       More Distress Selling
       More Reduction in Velocity
    V. *More Distress Selling*
       Contraction of Deposit Currency
       Further Dollar Enlargement (i.e., Deflation)
    VI. *Reduction in Net Worth*
       Increase in Bankruptcies
       More Pessimism and Distrust
       More Slowing in Velocity
       More Liquidation
    VII. *Decrease in Profits*
       Increase in Losses
       Increase in Pessimism
       Slower Velocity
       More Liquidation
       Reduction in Volume of Stock Trading
    VIII. *Decrease in Construction*
       Reduction in Output
       Reduction in Trade
       Unemployment
       More Pessimism
    IX. *Hoarding*
    X. *Runs on Banks*

Banks Curtailing Loans for Self-Protection
Banks Selling Investments
Bank Failures
Distrust Grows
More Hoarding
More Liquidation

He then went on to explain how, in such circumstance, the economy can become frozen in a liquidity trap:

If the over-indebtedness with which we started was great enough, the liquidation of debts cannot keep up with the fall of prices which it causes. In that case, the liquidation defeats itself. While it diminishes the number of dollars owed, it may not do so as fast as it increased the value of each dollar owed. Then, the very effort of individuals to lessen their burden of debts increases it, because of the mass effect of the stampede to liquidate in swelling each dollar owed. Then we have the great paradox which, I submit, is the chief secret of most if not all, great depressions: The more the debtors pay, the more they owe. The more the economic boat tips, the more it tends to tip. It is not tending to right itself, but is capsizing.

Fisher believed at that time (October 1933) that the economy was emerging out of depression because of President Roosevelt's New Deal policies, which he referred to as *artificial respiration*:

The depression out of which we are now (I trust) emerging is an example of a debt-deflation depression of the most serious sort. The debts of 1929 were the greatest known, both nominally and really, up to that time.

Had no "artificial respiration" been applied, we would soon have seen general bankruptcies of the mortgage guarantee companies, savings banks, life insurance companies, railways, municipalities, and states. By that time the Federal Government would probably have become unable to pay its bills without resort to the printing press, which would itself have been a very belated and unfortunate case of artificial respiration. If even then our rulers should still have insisted on "leaving recovery to nature" and should still have refused to inflate in any way, should vainly have tried to balance the budget and discharge more government employees, to raise taxes, to float, or try to float, more loans, they would soon have ceased to be our rulers. For we would have insolvency of our national government itself, and probably some form of political revolution without waiting for the next legal election.[2]

The economy did not emerge from depression in late 1933, however. The artificial respiration of the New Deal was too stop-and-start. The government stimulus made the economy revive when it was applied, but the patient lapsed back into crisis whenever the stimulus was withdrawn—the renewed downturn of 1938 followed the reduction in government spending in 1937.

Government stimulus on a much greater scale than either Fisher or Roosevelt imagined was required to end the depression—the stimulus of total war. That began, and the depression ended, in 1941.

It is quite possible that the New Depression will drag on for years just as the Great Depression did. The fiscal and monetary stimulus of 2009 to 2011 stopped the economy from spiraling into an across-the-board bankruptcy of all sectors, but it was not large enough—or rather, it was not spent in a clever enough way—to reignite sustainable growth. And now, as this book goes to print, the stimulus is being removed and the economic downturn is worsening again.

This stop-and-start pattern of stimulus and austerity, producing little booms and busts, may continue for years until finally the government's capacity to provide any more stimulus is exhausted. At that point, the deflationary death spiral will resume. However, there are no guarantees that events will unfold in that way. The government could remove all stimulus in the near term, resulting in a deflationary collapse in the near future. Or the government could go to the other extreme and provide so much stimulus, financed with fiat money creation, that the economy experiences high rates of inflation instead. Alternatively, a political swing toward protectionism, resulting in high trade tariffs, could also cause high rates of inflation.

There should be no doubt that the natural tendency for the economy—following a 40-year credit boom—is to collapse into a debt-deflation depression. Policy makers understand that. They have read Fisher's article. That is why they are determined to prevent that outcome from recurring. Try as they might, however, it is far from certain that they can prevent it. Moreover, their attempts to reflate the economy could go astray and actually generate very high rates of inflation or even hyperinflation. In that case, the cure could prove to be just as deadly as the disease.

Therefore, over the years ahead, the U.S. economy could suffer either severe debt-deflation or severe inflation. Either scenario would inflict enormous damage on the economy and, therefore, on society. However, the impact that deflation would have on asset prices would be very different from the impact that inflation would have.

Winners and Losers

It is well understood that inflation benefits debtors and that deflation (or mild deflation, at least) benefits creditors. Debtors gain when prices rise because their income increases but the amount of debt they owe remains unchanged. It becomes easier, therefore, for them to repay their debt. In periods of very high inflation, debt practically evaporates.

Creditors, of course, suffer from that process. Those who own bonds or who have money on deposit find that the purchasing power of their investments is eroded by rising prices. Hyperinflation can effectively destroy the savings of everyone not savvy enough to quickly move their wealth out of financial assets and into real assets.

So, who would the winners and losers be in each scenario?

The Fed's *Flow of Funds* Table L.1 provides a breakdown of TCMD by sector. It shows who owes the debt (the debtors) and who owns the debt (the creditors). In most cases, each sector has both credit market assets and credit market liabilities. Therefore, it is necessary to offset the assets and liabilities against each other in order to derive a net position.

On a net basis, as of mid-2011, *the federal government* has the largest net debt position, at $8.9 trillion. On the one hand, the government would therefore benefit from higher rates of inflation in the sense that inflation would cause its tax revenues to increase, making it easier for the government to repay the debt it had accumulated in the past. On the other hand, however, rising inflation would force the government to pay higher interest rates on the bonds it sold in the future. As a result, the amount of interest that the government would have to pay to finance its debt would rise. Higher interest payments would add to the budget deficit and further worsen the government's debt position. Very high inflation rates would be crippling. For instance, if the government were forced to pay 10 percent interest on its $8.9 trillion stock of debt, the interest expense alone would amount to $890 billion a year. Therefore, the government would not welcome high rates of inflation, despite being a large net debtor.

The household sector owes $13.3 trillion in debt, composed primarily of mortgage debt, $9.9 trillion, and consumer debt, $2.4 trillion. Offsetting that, it owns $4.1 trillion in credit market instruments and a further $8 trillion in deposits. Setting these liabilities and assets off against each other shows the household sector to have net debt of $1.2 trillion. Given that the rate of interest on at least some of the sector's consumer debt is floating rather than fixed, on balance, the household sector would not benefit significantly from rising prices despite the large amount of debt it has incurred in recent decades. Of course, the debt and the savings are not divided equally among all the households. Some families have much more debt than others, just as some have more savings than others. Inflation and deflation would therefore impact different households according to their individual financial positions.

The corporate sector would benefit from mild inflation. It owes $7.3 trillion in debt on a gross basis and more than $5 trillion on a net basis after deducting its credit market assets and its deposits. Moreover, businesses generally do benefit from mild inflation, which is thought to "grease the wheels" of the profit-making process. That is one of the reasons the Fed's inflation target rate is 2 percent rather than 0 percent.

The assets and liabilities of *the government-sponsored enterprises* (GSEs) roughly net off to zero, which suggests they would neither win nor lose from mild inflation or mild deflation. Finally, the sector described as *the rest of the world* (i.e., non-Americans) would clearly be harmed by inflation and would benefit from mild deflation. That sector is a net creditor to the amount of $6.1 trillion.

Ice Storm

Of course in severe debt-deflation almost everyone would lose because the financial system would collapse as a result of massive bankruptcies and defaults. Therefore, even the creditors would suffer as their assets were destroyed in the collapse of banks and other financial intermediaries. Those who hold large amounts of gold or cash would be in an advantageous position to buy up property and other real assets at very depressed prices. Those who own property and other real assets would find they were relatively much better off than the property-less majority. However, in the social upheaval that would likely ensue, it is uncertain whether property rights would continue to be respected. It is possible that a forced redistribution of property would take place. It is easy to see why policy makers are so determined to prevent such a course of events.

Fire Storm

In past periods of very high or hyperinflation, debtors and sophisticated speculators have been the beneficiaries at the expense of those with savings. Hyperinflation occurs when a currency is losing all or a great deal of its value against other currencies. Therefore, speculators profit from betting against the collapsing currency. Other types of speculation can also generate extraordinary profits. It is difficult to know in advance which investment would generate very high returns, however. Normally, very high rates of inflation only come about as the result of some extraordinary shock to the economy, such as war. Profits, therefore, are made by understanding the nature of each particular shock and making bets on which prices will rise most in those circumstances. The ability to borrow money at fixed interest rates is one of the surest paths to riches during a bout of severe inflation.

Wealth Preservation through Diversification

The hard truth is that it is not easy to preserve wealth. If it were, the families who were wealthy 200 years ago would still be wealthy today—and generally, they are not. In the very harsh economic environment that is likely to prevail over the next ten years, it is likely that a great deal of wealth is going to be destroyed. The economic system is in crisis and government policy, rather than market fundamentals, will determine the direction of asset prices. If the government fails to borrow and spend enough, the economy will collapse into a deflationary spiral. If it borrows, prints, and spends too much, there will be very high rates of inflation.

Future government policy simply cannot be foretold with any degrees of precision. Active wealth managers will have to rapidly adjust their portfolios in response to changes in policy. That will be no easy task, even for the experts. Those unable to devote all their time and energy to deciphering the kaleidoscopic changes in the politics and policies of Washington have the option of constructing a broadly diversified investment portfolio that would ensure significant wealth preservation regardless of whether the price level moves up or down.

The following are five components of a diversified portfolio:

1. *Commodities* generally perform well in an inflationary environment and suffer in times of disinflation or deflation. Gold and silver benefit most from quantitative easing, which undermines public confidence in the national currency.
2. *Stocks* tend to rise (1) in a healthy economic environment, (2) when central banks create money and pump it into the financial markets (so long as they don't cause too much inflation), (3) when the government runs a budget surplus and crowds in the private sector, and (4) when the trade deficit is larger than the budget deficit. The last two will be explained below. Stocks tend to perform badly when inflation at the CPI level exceeds 4 percent, in a weak economic environment, and, particularly, during a severe period of debt deflation.
3. *Bonds* benefit from disinflation or mild deflation and suffer when there is inflation. In the third quarter of 2011, the yield on ten-year government bonds fell to a record low of 1.7 percent. The Fed played a role in pushing the yields down by printing money and buying bonds. There was more to it than that, however. There was also a private sector flight to safety into government bonds as a result of fears that the Greek government would default on its debt, which would have resulted in a systemic banking crisis. Furthermore, U.S. yields seemed to be declining for the same reasons

that Japanese bond yields had fallen after Japan's economic bubble popped: the lack of viable investment opportunities elsewhere in the economy.

The yield on ten-year JGBs (Japanese government bonds) has fallen below 1 percent. It is possible that U.S. government bond yields will as well. However, the risk-reward tradeoff of investing in government bonds with such low yields appears highly unfavorable, particularly given the risk that inflation could easily move very much higher at some point during the next ten years.

4. *Rental property* can provide a relatively steady stream of income, although, as the experience of the last 15 years demonstrates, the capital value of the property can fluctuate widely. U.S. home prices have fallen by more than 30 percent on average since the crisis began and they could fall further, even significantly further in the case of a severe debt-deflation scenario. Even then, if well located, rental properties would continue to generate rental income. In a worse-case scenario, rents would fall significantly from current levels. If they do, however, most other prices would also tend to be much lower, leaving the owner relatively just as well off.

5. Financing rental properties with *fixed-interest-rate debt* adds a further element of portfolio diversification. Borrowing at fixed interest rates provides a hedge against inflation. Should inflation move higher, the rents would adjust upward, but the debt owed would remain the same, which would effectively reduce the burden of the debt. The risk, however, is that in a severe debt deflation, rents would fall so much that the rental income would be insufficient to service the mortgage. A prudent loan-to-value ratio mitigates that danger.

Those are the basic options: commodities (including gold and silver), stocks (preferably stocks with a good dividend yield), bonds, rental property, and fixed-interest-rate debt. In combination, they form a broadly diversified portfolio capable of preserving a significant amount of wealth in practically any conceivable economic environment.

During a period of high rates of inflation, the value of the bonds and the stocks would fall, but the price of the commodities would appreciate. Meanwhile, the rental property would continue to generate cash flow and the inflation-adjusted burden of debt would decline.

In case of deflation, commodity prices would fall. Stock prices would also fall, but the decline would be offset to some extent by dividend income. The value of the bonds in the portfolio would rise. And the rental income would continue to generate cash flow, although in lower amounts if rents adjust downward. Mortgage payments would remain unchanged.

Other Observations Concerning Asset Prices in the Age of Paper Money

Fiat money creation has begun to profoundly impact asset prices in recent years, often in ways that would not be expected.

Once Upon a Time in the West

Classical economic theory strove to explain the economic dynamics of a capitalist economy on a gold standard. Given that the current economic system is a government-directed system on a paper money standard, no one should be surprised that it does not behave as classical economic theory suggests a capitalist economy would. Thus far, there is no generally accepted theory of how this new system works—and, for that matter, there is very little general recognition that a new system exists at all.

Still, it is useful to understand how things were meant to work in the past when the economic system was capitalism. Two areas are of particular importance: government finance and international trade. An understanding of how they once worked helps clarify the consequences of how they work now.

First, in the past, government borrowing pushed up interest rates. Under a gold standard, there was a limited amount of money in an economy and governments could not create any more of it. Therefore, if governments borrowed money to finance a budget deficit, that pushed up interest rates and damaged the economy. That process was called *crowding out* because the government crowded the private sector out of the credit markets by making loans prohibitively expensive.

Second, international trade had to balance. If a country imported more than it exported, its gold was sent abroad to pay for the deficit. That caused the money supply to contract in the deficit country which, in turn, caused a recession, unemployment, and falling prices. Eventually, as domestic prices fell and as the unemployed bought less, the trade deficit came back into balance. In other words, there was an automatic adjustment mechanism under the gold standard that ensured that trade between nations balanced.

The economic system that emerged during the twentieth century is fundamentally different. Instead of forcing budgets and trade to balance, it finances the deficits. The manner in which they are financed has a profound and often unexpected impact on asset prices.

Money That Floats

First of all, consider currencies. By the end of the nineteenth century, only one currency was used across most of the developed world, gold.

Since countries could not manipulate gold's value, trade imbalances were resolved by market-determined adjustments to the price level of both countries. The deficit country experienced falling prices and the surplus country experienced inflation. Those price trends continued until the balance of trade was restored.

After the Bretton Woods system broke down in the early 1970s, however, currency values began to move up and down relative to one another—that is to say that currencies were floating rather than fixed. In this post–Bretton Woods arrangement, trade balances are the most important fundamental factor determining the long-term direction of exchange rate movements. A country with a trade surplus will normally experience an appreciating currency, while the currency of a country with a trade deficit will tend to depreciate. The appreciation of the yen from yen 360 to the U.S. dollar in the 1970s to yen 77 to the dollar in 2011 is a good example. Japan generally has a large trade surplus with the United States; therefore, its currency has naturally appreciated.

Over the short run, however, interest rate differentials are more important than trade balances in determining movements in exchange rates. If the central bank of one country raises the interest rate, the amount of money that can be earned by holding the currency of that country improves relative to what it was before. Therefore, that currency tends to attract more investors and, as a consequence, it appreciates relative to the value of the currencies of other countries that did not experience a rate increase.

During this economic crisis, however, a new factor has emerged that trumps trade balances and interest rate differentials in determining short-term currency movements. Now, fiat money creation is the most important factor. When the Fed, for instance, creates fiat money on a large scale as it did during QE1 and QE2, it puts downward pressure on the dollar's exchange rate because it increases the supply of dollars in the marketplace while the demand for dollars remains unchanged. The Fed, the Bank of England, the European Central Bank, and the Bank of Japan have all launched more than one round of quantitative easing in recent years.

Finally, there is also intervention by a central bank with the express purpose of fixing or moving a currency's value. China's central bank, for instance, does this on a daily basis to depress the value of the yuan. Other central banks intervene periodically to take currency speculators by surprise. Central banks intervene in the currency markets by creating the domestic currency and using it to buy the currency of a different country. The scale to which this occurs is reflected in the size of each country's foreign exchange reserves. The larger the reserves, the greater the intervention. Currency manipulation, therefore, can be measured by the size of a country's foreign exchange reserves.

The value of the currencies that are not pegged can be highly volatile. Moreover, short-term currency movements are notoriously difficult to predict.

Quantitative Easing and Asset Prices

The immediate effect of quantitative easing is to push interest rates down and to push stock prices and commodity prices up. As just mentioned, in a capitalist system, when a government borrowed money it pushed up interest rates. That is no longer necessarily the case. Today, interest rates are determined not only by the demand for money but also by the supply of money.

Consider the second round of quantitative easing. Between November 2010 and mid-2011, the Fed created $600 billion and used it to buy government bonds. That allowed the government to borrow money to finance its very large budget deficits without pushing up interest rates. The U.S. government needed to borrow a lot of money, so it printed a lot of money and lent it to itself. Had it not done so, it is likely that the government would have had to pay much higher interest rates to fund its 2011 budget deficit. Higher interest rates on government bonds would have pushed up all the other interest rates throughout the economy since government bonds act as the benchmark "risk-free" rate. Consequently, higher interest rates would have negatively impacted most sectors of the economy.

QE2 also pushed up stock prices, however. By buying $600 billion worth of government bonds, the Fed effectively financed the entire government budget deficit during those seven months. By doing so, it forced other investors who would have bought those bonds to buy something else. Some of the private sector money went into the stock market. As a result, there was a stock market rally that roughly corresponded with the life of QE2. Soon after the Fed stopped printing money and buying government bonds, stock prices fell.

Finally, QE2 also pushed up commodity prices. It is well understood that fiat money creation causes inflation. In fact, the Fed justified launching the second round of quantitative easing by citing the threat that deflation poised to the economy, implicitly admitting that it was creating fiat money in order to cause prices to rise. Food and energy prices moved significantly higher when QE2 began and then fell when it ended.

Therefore, the evidence is very persuasive that, at least over the short term, quantitative easing has the effect of pushing up the price of bonds, stocks, and commodities. And, when bond prices rise, their yield (i.e., interest rates) falls. However, had the Fed continued creating money over a much longer period, the consequences would most likely have been different. Commodity prices would have continued rising, but eventually, higher food and energy costs would have pushed the consumer price inflation index much higher, too. Fears of higher inflation would have frightened the bond market and caused interest rates to rise (and bond prices to fall). Higher interest rates would have also led to a stock market sell-off. Judging by the experience of the 1960s and 1970s, stocks perform badly when the inflation rate exceeds 4 percent. The Dow Jones Industrial Average could not break out above the 1,000 point level for 16 years so long as the CPI index remained above 4 percent.

Crowding In

During the late 1990s, the U.S. government actually had a budget surplus. Taxes had been increased twice earlier in the decade, once during the Bush administration and once during the Clinton administration. Military spending had also been curtailed following the end of the Cold War in 1989.

As a result, the government began paying down the national debt, rather than selling more debt each year as it had normally done for decades. The government took its budget surplus and bought back the bonds it had sold to the public in the past. That disrupted the normal flows of the financial markets.

When the government bought back its bonds from the private sector, the private sector was left with more cash. Furthermore, because the government was not selling new bonds every year, government debt ceased to soak up the economy's growing pool of investable capital as it typically did. Combined those two factors meant there was a great deal more liquidity sloshing around the financial markets than normal. Some of that liquidity went into the stock market and fueled the absurd surge in stock prices that occurred at that time. The government's budget surplus and its repayment of government debt "crowded in" the private sector and produced the fin de la siècle NASDAQ bubble. (See Exhibit 10.1.)

The Budget Deficit, the Trade Deficit, and Asset Prices

The size of the U.S. trade deficit relative to the size of the U.S. budget deficit has a profound impact on asset prices. That is because the trade deficit determines the size of the U.S. financial account surplus (i.e., the size of the capital inflows into the United States). When those inflows are larger than the budget deficit, interest rates tend to fall and asset prices tend to rise.

When the United States has a trade deficit, that deficit throws dollars off into the global economy. The central banks of the corresponding trade surplus countries generally buy those dollars in order to prevent their currencies from appreciating. If they did not, the conversion of the dollars into the currency of the surplus country would cause the latter to appreciate, which would damage that country's export sector. Once the central banks have

EXHIBIT 10.1 U.S. Budget Surpluses and Deficits

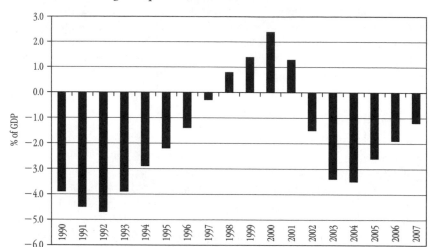

Source: Office of Management and Budget

bought the dollars, they need to invest them into U.S. dollar-denominated assets in order to earn an investment return. U.S. government bonds are the preferred investment choice for central banks because they are considered to be risk-free.

When the U.S. trade deficit is larger than the U.S. budget deficit, however, as was the case from 1996 to 2008, the U.S. government does not issue enough bonds to absorb all the dollars that the central banks would like to invest. That forces the central banks to buy other U.S. dollar-denominated assets. If they buy the government bonds that had been sold in earlier years, that pushes up bond prices and pushes down interest rates. If they buy GSE debt, that pushes up property prices when the GSEs invest that cash into mortgages. If they buy stocks, that contributes to a stock market rally. In any case, when the U.S. trade deficit (and, therefore, the U.S. financial account surplus) is larger than the government's budget deficit, it puts downward pressure on interest rates and upward pressure on asset prices. That was the case for 12 straight years from 1996 to 2008; and that was one of the primary causes of the asset price bubbles that did such damage to the health of the U.S. economy over that period. (See Exhibit 10.2.)

Once the crisis began, the trade deficit was no longer large enough to finance the greatly expanded budget deficit. The gap between the two was $1 trillion in 2009, $814 billion in 2010, and will be roughly $800 billion in 2011, a cumulative shortfall of $2.6 trillion. Quantitative easing was required to plug that gap. The Fed expanded its balance sheet by approximately $2 trillion over those three years.

EXHIBIT 10.2 The U.S. Budget Deficit and the U.S. Current Account Deficit

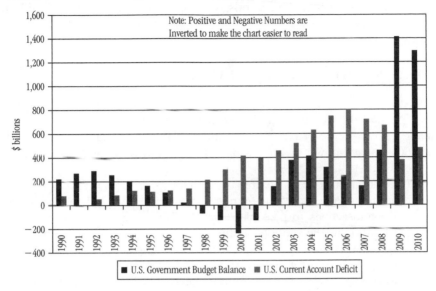

Source: Congressional Budget Office and Bureau of Economic Analysis

Looking ahead, the government's budget deficit is likely to remain significantly larger than the U.S. trade deficit for many years. Consequently, additional rounds of quantitative easing should be anticipated. More fiat money will be required to finance the budget deficit if interest rates are to remain low.

In the unlikely event that the budget deficit declines at the same time that the trade deficit expands, a new round of asset price inflation would likely ensue.

For these reasons, it is important to monitor the gap between the budget deficit and the trade deficit.

Protectionism and Inflation

The unemployment crisis in the United States is very likely to produce a virulent political backlash against free trade during the years ahead. If import tariffs are enacted, there will be a sharp rise in inflation. The tariff rate would immediately feed through to higher consumer prices. Moreover, industrial bottlenecks would emerge as the country begins to manufacture more domestically.

The importation of goods made with low-cost labor has been an indispensable component of the credit-driven economic system that has taken shape in the United States in recent decades. That system would not survive if trade barriers were erected. High rates of inflation would drive interest rates sharply higher. Bonds, stocks, and property prices would all crash as a result.

Consequences of Regulating Derivatives

The chances are quite high that the prices of some commodities are being manipulated through the derivatives market. In fact, given the size of the market, the volume of transactions, the fact that it is largely unregulated, and all that is known of human nature, it would be naïve to ignore this possibility.

Legislation has been enacted (The Dodd–Frank Wall Street Reform and Consumer Protection Act) to regulate this industry and to force most derivative transactions to take place through exchanges. If those laws are enforced—and they have not been thus far—the increased transparency they would provide could expose a great deal of inappropriate or illegal trading activity. If manipulation is occurring through the derivatives market, the enforcement of the new regulations could cause a sharp decline in the price of a number of important commodities. That risk bears monitoring.

Conclusion

There is extreme disequilibrium in the global economy. Too much credit has caused too much industrial capacity and has driven asset prices far above the level that can be supported by the income of the general population.

Government debt and massive fiat money creation has succeeded in perpetuating this disequilibrium since the crisis began in 2008. It is uncertain how much longer those measures can be sustained. Should they cease altogether, there would be a horrible debt-deflation similar—in cause and consequence—to that which occurred during the Great Depression. Government attempts to prevent that outcome, or political developments that drive policy in a harmful direction, could go astray and produce the opposite effect, very high rates of inflation.

Given that the price level could either collapse or surge higher, it is necessary to be prepared for either scenario. It is also important to keep in mind that "market fundamentals" are no longer the only determinants of price movements. In the twenty-first century, various forms of government intervention frequently have an even greater impact.

Supply and demand are still the ultimate arbitrators of value. Today, however, governments often have an extraordinary influence on both.

Notes

1. From *The Constitution of Liberty* (Chicago: University of Chicago Press, 1960), p. 338.
2. Irving Fisher, "The Debt-Deflation Theory of Great Depressions," *Econometrica* (October 1933).

Conclusion

This is the third book I have written on the crisis in the global economy. *The Dollar Crisis*, published in March 2003, explained why the crisis was inevitable given the flaws in the post–Bretton Woods international monetary system. *The Corruption of Capitalism*, December 2009, discussed the long series of U.S. policy mistakes that led to this disaster. This book focuses specifically on the role that credit expansion has played in shaping what appears to be an unsustainable economic paradigm. It also provides a simple analytical framework, the quantity theory of credit, that clarifies all the important aspects of our emergency. Simply put, an unprecedented expansion of credit, made possible by the adoption of fiat money 40 years ago, has reshaped the global economy and fundamentally altered the economic system itself. Our civilization has been built on $50 trillion of credit and is now teetering on the brink of bankruptcy because too much of that credit has been misallocated and cannot be repaid.

Economic crises of this magnitude become political crises. The societal bargains that have been struck since the late 1960s—the expansion of Medicare, Social Security, military spending, and government-funded corporate welfare—have been financed on credit. If those promises can no longer be fulfilled, a convulsive political upheaval will occur.

From a great distance, human history looks much like rival microscopic organisms doing battle in a petri dish. Actions taken for reasons of economic exigency have always been justified on religious or ideological grounds. Napoleon's conquest of Europe grew out of the bankruptcy of the ancient regime and the monetary chaos of the French Revolution. Japan's invasion of Asia and Germany's occupation of Europe during the 1930s and 1940s resulted from the economic upheavals released by World War I and the Great Depression. If our credit-based economic system fails, a geopolitical cataclysm is sure to follow.

The analysis I presented in my first two books was well received; my recommendations generally were not. In *The Dollar Crisis*, I proposed (1) a global minimum wage, structured to increase wages in the manufacturing sector by $1 per day each year; and (2) the use of IMF Special Drawing Rights (SDRs) to boost international liquidity when the crisis struck. Had the minimum wage proposal been adopted at that time, wage rates in the developing world would have practically tripled by now to $14 per day, thereby tripling the purchasing power of those workers near the bottom of the labor pyramid. The aggregate demand thus created would have offset the collapse in demand that resulted from the deflation of the U.S. property bubble. The second recommendation, although initially controversial, was, in fact, implemented. The supply of SDRs was increased by a factor of 10 in 2009 and it is very likely to be expanded again soon in response to the sovereign debt crisis in Europe.

In *The Corruption of Capitalism*, I recommended that the United States government invest $3 trillion in twenty-first-century technologies over ten years in order to restructure the U.S. economy and restore its economic viability. Since then, the government has spent $2 trillion more in ways that have temporarily boosted consumption and prevented economic collapse, without doing anything meaningful to resolve the country's structural crisis. Meanwhile, public mistrust of the government has increased, and a powerful grassroots political movement demanding less government spending has captured the Republican Party.

This book is an appeal to the public to think again. *Austerity* means collapse—the collapse of the social contract within the United States and the collapse of U.S. military hegemony abroad. The ultimate consequences of that scenario are unpredictable, but certain to be dire.

That course is unnecessary and avoidable. Our economic system requires credit expansion in order to generate economic growth. The household sector cannot bear any additional debt, but the government sector can. If government spending is to be sustainable, however, the government must change the way it spends. Rather than spending trillions of dollars each year in a manner that only boosts consumption, the government must begin to invest in large-scale projects that can generate a return. The government can now borrow at 2 percent interest. If it borrows at 2 percent, invests and earns 3 percent, our national emergency will lessen. If it borrows at 2 percent and invests in transformative mega-projects, such as the development of solar energy, this crisis will be overcome and prosperity for the next generation will be assured.

The economic system that has grown out of the adoption of fiat money is new. It is different from what came before. It is not capitalism. We have not yet learned how it works. Its weaknesses have become glaringly apparent. Yet we are ignoring the possibilities it presents. What a tragic mistake it would be to impose austerity and see our world implode, when so much credit is available at ultra low costs. All that is required is for us, as a society, to invest that credit imaginatively. If we do, we can achieve global economic prosperity beyond the dreams of all earlier generations.

About the Author

Richard Duncan is the author of two earlier books on the global economic crisis. *The Dollar Crisis: Causes, Consequences, Cures* (2003) explained why a worldwide economic calamity was inevitable given the flaws in the post–Bretton Woods international monetary system. It was an international bestseller. *The Corruption of Capitalism* (2009) described the long series of U.S. policy mistakes responsible for the crisis. It also outlined the policies necessary to permanently resolve it.

Since beginning his career as an equities analyst in Hong Kong in 1986, Richard has served as global head of investment strategy at ABN AMRO Asset Management in London, worked as a financial sector specialist for the World Bank in Washington, DC, and headed equity research departments for James Capel Securities and Salomon Brothers in Bangkok. He also worked as a consultant for the IMF in Thailand during the Asia Crisis. He is now chief economist at Blackhorse Asset Management in Singapore.

Richard studied economics and literature at Vanderbilt University (1983) and international finance at Babson College (1986). Between the two, he spent a year traveling around the world as a backpacker.

Please visit the author's website, Economics in the Age of Paper Money: http://www.richardduncaneconomics.com/

Index

Agency-backed mortgage pools,
  35–37, 69
AIG, 48, 68, 86
Alternative fiscal scenario, of
  Congressional Budget Office,
  141–142
American Solar initiative, proposed,
  143–145
America's Great Depression
  (Rothbard), 64, 138–139
Asset-Backed Commercial Paper
  Money Mutual Market Fund
  Liquidity Facility (AMLF), 68
Asset-backed securities (ABSs),
  11–12, 88
Asset prices:
  inflation and deflation and, 60,
    155–165
  quantitative easing and, 76–77,
    162–163, 164
Austerity program option, for U.S.,
  143, 155, 170

Balance of payments:
  asset prices and, 163–165
  currencies and, 160–162
  foreign central banks' creation
    of fiat money and foreign
    exchange reserves, 17–28
  global imbalances, 83,
    101–104
  government finance and, 160

quantitative easing and, 75–76
  U.S. and foreign exchange
    reserves, 81–83
Banking sector:
  commercial banks, credit
    creation, and decline in
    liquidity reserves, 5–9
  commercial banks' credit
    structure, 10–12
  current financial health of,
    96–101
  in Mitchell's theory of business
    cycles, 108
  New Great Depression scenarios
    and, 126
Bank of America, 48, 97–100
Baruch, Bernard, 134
Bear Stearns, 48, 68
Bernanke, Ben:
  global savings glut theory of, 18,
    19, 28–32
  on Milton Friedman, 66, 77
  policy responses to credit
    expansion and New Depression,
    63, 70, 72, 113
Bodin, Jean, 52
Bonds:
  in diversified portfolio, 158–159
  effect of stimulus on, 117
  quantitative easing and, 114,
    162–163
Bush, George W., 105

Business cycles, theories of, 64,
    107–109
*Business Cycles: The Problem and
    Its Setting* (Mitchell), 108–109

Capital adequacy ratio (CAR), 9, 12
Capitalism, evolution to credit-
    based, government-directed
    economic system, 133–139
China:
    fiat money creation and foreign
        exchange reserves, 20–24,
        29–31, 78–80, 103, 161
    New Great Depression scenarios
        and, 127, 130–131
    possibility of end to buying of
        U.S. debt, 31–32
Citibank, 97–100
Commercial banks. *See*
    Banking sector
Commercial Paper Funding Facility
    (CPFF), 68
Commodities:
    in diversified portfolio, 158–159
    inflation and, 60
    quantitative easing and, 162–163
    regulation of derivatives market
        and, 166
Congressional Budget Office
    (CBO):
    budget outlook scenarios, 140–142
    government debt estimates,
        94–95
Construction sector, in Mitchell's
    theory of business cycles, 108
Consumer price inflation, 60
Corporate sector:
    inflation and deflation's effects
        on, 156–157
    share of U.S. debt, 34
Corruption of Capitalism, The
    (Duncan), 169, 170

Credit creation and expansion:
    credit structure of U.S., 1945 and
        2007, 10–11
    economic growth and, 86–88
    essential to booms, 64, 109
    foreign causes, 13, 15, 17–32
    transformation of U.S. economy
        by, 33–49
    U.S. domestic causes, 1–15
"Crowding in," 163
"Crowding out," 74, 160
Currencies, trade balances and,
    160–162
Current account balances. *See*
    Balance of payments

"Debt-Deflation Theory of Great
    Depressions, The" (Fisher),
    151–155
Deflation. *See* Inflation and deflation
Deindustrialization, 103–104, 120
Demand deposits, commercial bank
    funding and, 7–8
Democratic Party, 105, 114
Derivatives:
    consequences of regulating,
        126, 166
    U.S. banks' exposure to, 97–101
Diversification, of investment
    portfolio, 158–159
Dodd–Frank Wall Street Reform and
    Consumer Protection Act, 99,
    166
Dollar Crisis, The (Duncan), 169–170
Domestic causes, of credit
    expansion, 1–15
    Federal Reserve, end of gold
        standard, and creation of fiat
        money, 1–4
    financial sector and lack of
        liquidity reserve requirements,
        5–15

Dow Jones Industrial Average, 39–40, 71–72, 163

Economic growth. *See* Credit creation and expansion
Economies, major components of, 73–75. *See also* U.S. economy
Election of 2012, issues of government spending and indebtedness, 112–113
Emotions, in Mitchell's theory of business cycles, 108
Energy and energy prices. *See also* Solar initiative, proposed
  excluded from CPI, 60
  in New Great Depression, 130
  quantitative easing and, 77, 119, 162
England, 102, 131
Equation of exchange, 52–55
European Central Bank, 78
Extended-baseline scenario, of Congressional Budget Office, 140–141

Fannie Mae:
  conservatorship of, 36, 68, 86, 101
  credit creation and decline in liquidity reserves, 11–13, 138
  quantitative easing and, 69
  U.S. debt guarantees and, 26–28, 35–37, 95
FDIC, 96–97
Federal Reserve. *See also* Quantitative easing
  commercial bank reserves (1945–2007), 8–9
  end of gold standard, creation of fiat money, and expansion of credit, 1–4
  policy actions regarding New Depression, 63–83

Federal Reserve Act of 1913, 3, 5
Fiat money:
  end of gold standard and creation of, 1–4
  government deficit in 2013 and 2014 and, 117
Fiat Money Inflation in France (White), 128
Financial sector:
  debt and, 34–37, 92–93
  lack of liquidity reserve requirements and credit expansion, 5–15, 88
Fiscal stimulus, needed with additional quantitative easing, 114–119
Fisher, Irving, 52–55, 58
  theory of debt-deflation, 151–155
Fixed-interest-rate debt, in diversified portfolio, 159
Flow of Funds Accounts of the United States, 13–15, 156
Food prices:
  deflation and, 151
  excluded from CPI, 60
  quantitative easing and, 77, 114, 116, 118–119, 131–132, 162
Foreign causes, of credit expansion, 13, 15, 17–32
  Bernanke's global savings glut theory and, 18, 19, 28–31
  central banks' creation of fiat money and foreign exchange reserves, 17–28
  possibility of end to China's buying of U.S. debt, 31–32
Foreign exchange reserves. *See* Balance of payments
Fortune magazine, 89–90
Fractional reserve banking, money creation through, 5–7, 10

Freddie Mac:
   conservatorship of, 36, 68,
      86, 101
   credit creation and decline in
      liquidity reserves, 11–13, 138
   quantitative easing and, 69
   U.S. debt guarantees and, 26–28,
      35–37, 95
Friedman, Milton, 55, 63, 66,
      70, 77

General equilibrium, theory of,
      107–108
Germany, 102, 125, 131
Glass–Steagall Act, 7
Globalization, 22, 55–56, 60, 91–92,
      110, 116–117, 119, 139
Global savings glut theory, of
      Bernanke, 18, 19, 28–32
Goldman Sachs, 47–48
Gold reserve requirement,
      end of and creation of fiat
      money, 1–4
Government Accountability Office
      report, 68
Government sector:
   inflation and deflation's effects
      on, 156
   percentage of total credit market
      debt, 93–96
   rational investment option for,
      143–145, 170
   results of spending cuts in, 74–75
Government-sponsored entities
      (GSEs):
   credit supply and, 11–13
   GSE-backed mortgage pools, 35–37
   inflation and deflation's effects
      on, 157
   quantitative easing and, 69–71
   U.S. debt guarantees and, 26–28,
      35–37
Great Depression, 97, 110, 151

economic conditions during,
      121–126
Friedman's conclusions about,
      63, 66
Greece, 102
Greenspan, Alan, 19, 63, 66, 89–91
Gross domestic product (GDP):
   change in value added, by
      industry, 41–43
   debt as percentage of, 38–39,
      46–49, 73–74, 137, 140
   driven by credit, 58
   equation of exchange and,
      53–54
   during Great Depression, 122, 124
   ratio of credit growth to, 2,
      117–119
GSE-backed mortgage pools, 35–37

History of Economic Analysis
      (Schumpeter), 52
Hoover, Herbert, 122
Household sector:
   debt and, 34, 37–40, 88–92,
      110, 133
   inflation and deflation's effects
      on, 156
Human Action (von Mises), 64
Hyperinflation, 128, 155, 156, 157

Inflation and deflation, 149–166
   credit and inflation, 59–61
   derivative regulation and, 166
   effects on asset classes, 155–165
   Fisher's theory of debt-deflation,
      151–155
   inflation in 2011, 111–112
   inflation likely in 2012, 112–114
   inflation likely without additional
      quantitative easing and fiscal
      stimulus, 116–119
   New Great Depression scenarios
      and, 126

protectionism and, 155, 165–166
wealth preservation during,
158–159
Innovation, in Mitchell's theory of
business cycles, 108
Interest rates, in U.S.:
bond sales and, 26
cut by Federal Reserve to
encourage credit expansion,
66–67
money supply and, 74, 162–163
quantitative easing and, 76–77
trade balances and, 161
International Monetary Fund, 78
Ireland, 102

Jackson, Andrew, 151
Japan, 24, 29, 30, 82, 94, 96, 110,
116, 117, 125, 128, 130, 131,
140, 159, 161
Johnson, Lyndon, 1, 3
JP Morgan, 48
JPMorgan Chase, 97–100

Keynes, John Maynard, 104, 105
Korea, 29, 30, 128, 131

Labor market, changes in marginal
cost of wages in, 55, 60,
150–151, 165–166, 170. *See also*
Unemployment
Laissez-faire capitalism, evolution
to credit-based, government-
directed economic system,
133–139
Lehman Brothers, 48, 68
Libertarian Party, 105, 139
Life insurance companies, credit
supply and, 10–12

Maiden Lane I, I, and III, 68
Marx, Karl, 135
Merrill Lynch, 48

Military sector, in New Great
Depression, 129–130
Mitchell, Wesley, 108–109
Monetarism, 51, 55–57
Monetary aggregates, 56
*Monetary History of the United
States, 1967–1960, A*
(Friedman and Schwartz), 66
Money market funds, credit supply
and, 12
Money multiplier, 5, 7
Money supply, during Great
Depression, 121–122
Morgan Stanley, 48
Mutual funds, credit supply and, 12

Net worth, credit expansion's effect
on, 39–40
New Deal, 122–125, 135, 154–155
New Depression, 85–105
banking sector and, 96–101
global trade imbalances and,
101–104
policy responses to, 63–83
private sector debt and, 85–96
New Great Depression. *See also*
Inflation and deflation
consequences of, 128–132
policy options to prevent,
133–146
scenarios leading to, 126–128
Nixon, Richard, 103

Obama, Barack, 105
Oil prices. *See* Energy and energy
prices
Overproduction, in Mitchell's theory
of business cycles, 108

Paul, Ron, 139
People's Bank of china (PBOC),
21–22, 29–30, 78
Perot, Ross, 127

Primary dealer credit facility
  (PDCF), 68
Private sector debt:
  contraction of, 110–112
  effect of stimulus on, 117, 118
Production incomes, in Mitchell's
  theory of business cycles, 108
Profits:
  credit expansion's effect on,
    41, 42
  in Mitchell's theory of business
    cycles, 109
Property rights, debt-deflation
  and, 157
Protectionism:
  inflation and, 155, 165–166
  New Great Depression scenarios
    and, 127–128
Purchasing Power of Money: Its
  Determination and Relation to
  Credit, Interest and Crises, The
  (Fisher), 52–55

Quantitative easing:
  asset prices and, 76–77,
    162–163, 164
  balance of payments and,
    75–76
  beginning of, 68–69
  QE1, 9, 49, 67, 69–71, 74, 75–76
  QE2, 72–76
  QE3, 111–119
Quantity theory of credit, 51–61
  banking sector crisis and,
    126–127
  monetarism and, 55–57
  principles of, 57–61
  quantity theory of money
    contrasted, 52–55
  uses of, 51–52
Quantity theory of money, 51,
  52–57

Rational investment option, for
  U.S., 143
  solar initiative example,
    143–145, 170
Reagan, Ronald, 87–88, 105,
  138, 150
Rental property, in diversified
  portfolio, 159
Republican Party, 105, 112,
  120, 170
Reserve requirements:
  asset-based securities and
    government-sponsored entities
    and, 11–15
  commercial banks and, 5–9
  current, 8
Roosevelt, Franklin D., 122, 125,
  135, 154–155
Rothbard, Murray, 64, 134–135,
  138–139
Russia, 131

Saving and investment, in
  Mitchell's theory of business
  cycles, 108
Savings and loan companies, credit
  supply and, 10–12
Schumpeter, Joseph, 52, 53
Schwartz, Anna Jacobson, 66
Solar initiative, proposed,
  143–145, 170
Spain, 102, 125
Special Drawing Rights
  (SDRs), 78
Special purpose vehicles (SPVs),
  credit creation and, 12
Status quo option, for U.S., 143
Stocks:
  in diversified portfolio, 158–159
  quantitative easing and, 76–77,
    114, 162–163
Switzerland, 80–81

Taiwan, 29, 30–31
Tariffs:
  inflation and, 155, 165–166
  New Great Depression scenarios
    and, 127
Tax revenues:
  credit expansion's effect on,
    41, 42
  during Great Depression,
    124–125
  New Great Depression
    consequences and, 128
Theory of Money and Credit,
  The (von Mises), 64
Time deposits, commercial bank
  funding and, 7–8
Total credit market debt (TCMD):
  contraction of, 65
  by economic sector, 89–96
  foreign central banks' creation
    of fiat money and foreign
    exchange reserves, 17–28
  in 2011, 111–112
  likely for 2012, 112–113
  major categories of, 13–14
  sectors and changing percentages
    of debt, 33–38
Trade, generally. *See also* Balance
  of payments
  during Great Depression,
    122, 123
  in New Great Depression, 130

Uncertainty, in Mitchell's theory of
  business cycles, 108
Unemployment, 31, 73, 75,
  85–86, 92
  during Great Depression,
    122–124
  inflation and deflation's effects
    on, 149, 152, 165
  New Great Depression scenarios
    and, 112, 115–116, 126–127,
    130–131
U.S. economy, credit expansion
  and:
  impact on capital structure,
    45–49
  impact on economy, 38–45
  sectors and changing percentages
    of debt, 33–38

Volcker, Paul, 150
Von Mises, Ludwig, 63, 64, 109,
  138, 139

Wages. *See* Labor market
Walras, Leon, 107
Weather, in Mitchell's theory of
  business cycles, 108
Wells Fargo Bank, 97–99
White, Andrew, 128
World War II, 122–125, 134–135
  government spending and,
    135–137